D0593423

The Gospel according to
The Simpsons,™
Bigger and Possibly Even Better! Edition

The Gospel according to *The Simpsons*,™ Bigger and Possibly Even Better! Edition

Leader's Guide for Group Study

Samuel F. (Skip) Parvin
and Mark I. Pinsky

WJK WESTMINSTER
JOHN KNOX PRESS
LOUISVILLE · KENTUCKY

© 2009 Samuel F. "Skip" Parvin and Mark I. Pinsky

First edition
Published by Westminster John Knox Press
Louisville, Kentucky

09 10 11 12 13 14 15 16 17 18—10 9 8 7 6 5 4 3 2 1

Scripture quotations from the New Revised Standard Version of the Bible are copyright © 1989 by the Division of Christian Education of the National Council of the Churches of Christ in the U.S.A. and are used by permission.

Book design by Sharon Adams
Cover design by Teri Vinson

Library of Congress Cataloging-in-Publication Data

Pinsky, Mark I.
　　The gospel according to the Simpsons : bigger and possibly even better! edition : leader's guide for group study / Mark I. Pinsky and Samuel F. "Skip" Parvin.—2nd ed.
　　　　p. cm.
　　ISBN 978-0-664-23208-5 (alk. paper)
　　1. Simpsons (Television program)—Study guides. 2. Television broadcasting—Religious aspects. I. Parvin, Samuel F., 1953– II. Title.
　　PN1992.77.S58P55 2009
　　791.45'72—dc22

2009006574

PRINTED IN THE UNITED STATES OF AMERICA

∞ The paper used in this publication meets the minimum requirements of the American National Standard for Information Sciences—Permanence of Paper for Printed Library Materials, ANSI Z39.48-1992.

Westminster John Knox Press advocates the responsible use of our natural resources. The text paper of this book is made from 30% post-consumer waste.

Contents

Family Guy

King of the Hill

Introduction to the Second Edition

Much has changed and much has remained the same in the years since the first edition of this unlikely guide was conceived and published. Hundreds of churches and college youth groups have used animated comedies to introduce and instruct young people on issues of faith and values. Some have used this guide; others have developed their own variations. Spiritual elements seasoned *The Simpsons Movie*, whose worldwide gross at the box office and DVD sales so far have approached a billion dollars. The fact that *The Simpsons* are in fact a religious—if not always spiritual—family has become so widely accepted that their Christian faith was an answer in a recent *Jeopardy* season. What greater barometer of culture acceptance in modern American could there be?

Other cartoon shows aimed at adolescents and younger adults have streamed through the door that *The Simpsons* has kicked open, making religion, faith, and spirituality acceptable comedic elements, which is why we have added chapters in this edition on *Futurama*, *Family Guy*, and *King of the Hill*. A session on *The Simpsons Movie* and the environmental film *An Inconvenient Truth* has also been added—perfect for a weekend retreat or lock-in with youth.

Other shows, such as *American Dad* and, yes, *South Park*, have also made sometimes challenging (and often repulsive) use of the issues of religion, faith, and spirituality over the last decade. In 2009, *Family Guy* devoted most of an episode to a sympathetic portrayal of atheism—the witty, alcoholic dog Brian comes out of the closet as an atheist—and the intolerant reaction of the religious believers of Quahog, including his own family. And, in a fantasy "Treehouse of Horrors" episode, Homer comes back from the dead with the revelation that the one true faith is actually a mix of voodoo and "a form of Methodism." Who, other than mainline zombies, would have suspected?

There is no telling how long new episodes of *The Simpsons* will be produced, or whether there will be any more feature films. But given the enduring appeal of the show, and the development of more accessible technologies, it is probably safe to say that, like the poor, *The Simpsons* will always be with us.

Mark I. Pinsky

Introduction to the First Edition

I am a committed Jew, despite the earnest ministrations of legions of well-meaning, evangelical Christians. So I might not be the first person you think of to help design a Sunday school curriculum guide—even one based on a book that I wrote. Nonetheless, when I was a religion writer in the heart of the American Sunbelt, I think I probably spent more time in church each month than lots of Christians. And one thing I have learned for certain from this reporting is how important religious leaders—clergy and lay—believe it is to communicate the importance of faith and belief to teens and young adults. A consensus seems to be forming in this country that popular culture may be one avenue to reach people not otherwise inclined to church, if only by stealth. Maybe it's because I write a lot about the intersection of religion and popular culture, but I seem to see evidence of this trend everywhere.

Consider: On a Sunday night in December 2001, a cartoon character in a popular prime-time television sitcom, distraught over changes at the Protestant church where her family worships every week, decides to convert to Buddhism. The episode was appropriately titled "She of Little Faith." At the same time this episode of *The Simpsons* aired, on another network, *Touched by an Angel* dramatized the story of a woman who lost a friend in the September 11 terrorist attacks. Paralyzed with fear and anxiety, the woman is visited by an angel who assures her that God will be with her always. A week later—by popular demand—an episode of the comedy-drama *Ally McBeal* was repeated in which the title character tries to comfort a minister whose faith is shaken by his wife's murder. Don't be shocked. These episodes are not an aberration for commercial television, long considered the devil's playground.

Little by little, Hollywood writers and producers are discovering that faith may actually have some entertainment value. For decades—and for a number of complex reasons, mostly involving fear of offending—prime-time programming has consistently avoided religion. This despite the fact that, according to pollsters from George Gallup to George Barna, faith forms such a large part of the lives of most Americans on the other side of the screen.

"It is something new, because religion is the last frontier that commercial television was willing to foray into," says Robert Thompson, professor of media and popular culture at Syracuse University. "Religion was the one place that they pretty much steered clear of. Popular culture was supposed to comfort people. Religion, the idea went, made people uncomfortable. Television executives felt that if they reflected the real world in prime-time entertainment, then people would reject it. They really believed that entertainment was an anesthesia to what was going on in the news."

Of course, not all academics agree. "Religion comes and goes on prime time, depending on Hollywood folklore about what attracts audiences," says Quentin Schultze, professor of communication at Calvin College, an evangelical Christian school in Grand Rapids, Michigan. "When the economy goes into a tailspin or something horrendous happens in the news—like the September 11 disasters—television and film writers sense that spirituality is important to people."

In recent television seasons, this cyclical role of religion on television has begun to change, perhaps fundamentally, with the ratings success (or at least survival) of shows built around religion and spirituality, such as *Touched By an Angel* and *7th Heaven*. Viewers have signaled their willingness to accept a devout bailiff in

Judging Amy, a goofy but believing brother on *Maybe It's Me*, and a praying (if argumentative) president in *The West Wing*. Even on the scatological *South Park*, Jesus wrestles with Satan—winning only because the Prince of Darkness bets against himself and throws the fight.

"What entertainment producers have figured out, and what some religious leaders are still struggling to comprehend, is that this religion is increasingly pluralistic and less tied to creed and dogma," says Teresa Blythe, coauthor of *Watching What We Watch: Prime-Time Television through the Lens of Faith*. "That's why we see story lines involving a lot of different religions. As it became fashionable to portray Buddhist or New Age spirituality, it became more acceptable to portray all varieties of Christian spirituality."

What is going on here? This is a long way from *M*A*S*H*'s ineffectual Catholic chaplain, Father Mulcahy. Should Bill Moyers be concerned that the commercial networks are encroaching on his PBS turf? "Hardly," says Blythe. "Commercial networks exist for one reason—to make money. They will most likely use religion in story lines or documentaries only to the point that it helps sell advertising time. As soon as religion starts stepping on toes and demanding economic justice for all, television will pull back." Schultze agrees, to an extent, but he sees other problems.

"There's more than enough room for gaggles of religious characters and plots on mainstream television," he says. "The problem is not whether audiences are interested in spiritual matters, but rather the fact that so many writers and producers don't have religious experiences to call upon. Hollywood is not the most devout place on the planet."

There is little debate over the value and power of popular culture in providing moral, if not religious, instruction for young children. Think about the messages and lessons about good always being rewarded and evil always punished that are presented in Walt Disney's animated features, such as *Snow White* and *Pinocchio*. More recently, Disney's *Lion King* video, with its "great circle of life" philosophy, sold tens of millions of copies after having made hundreds of millions of dollars at the box office. DreamWorks's *Prince of Egypt*, the story of Moses and the exodus, was hailed by religious leaders across the theological spectrum, many of whom were consulted on the production of the animated feature. And the cartoon images don't have to move to deliver their message. Comic strip writers are no longer hesitant to draw on the divine. Although pioneered by Charles Schulz in *Peanuts*, religious references are now as likely to show up in modern strips such as *Rose Is Rose* and *Wildwood* as they are in more venerable strips such as *Dennis the Menace*, *B.C.*, *Beetle Bailey*, and *Family Circus*.

"Comedy and faith are natural partners in storytelling," says Calvin's Professor Schultze. "Comedy shows us how silly we are, the crazy situations we get ourselves into even when we are trying to be good. Just as television is the nation's jester, the daily comics are our one-minute homilies. The comics are about our foolishness—even how we survive with grace."

Clearly something is at work, because the growing traffic between religion and popular culture seems to be traveling in both directions. In increasing numbers, American religious leaders are turning to popular culture to communicate their theological values. "Television and film producers are the modern-day storytellers who have to stay in touch with what viewers believe is important, which includes religion. They don't always get it right, but the fact that they have noticed that viewers can not only take religious subject matter but actually enjoy it has energized some religious leaders in this country—at least those willing to recognize that popular culture matters," says Blythe. Christian study Bibles and Sunday school curricula—such as the one you are about to read—have already been developed based on such 1960s and 1970s television staples as *The Andy Griffith Show*, *The Beverly Hillbillies*, and *The Brady Bunch*. Syracuse's Thompson, himself a former Sunday school teacher at his Presbyterian church, sees nothing wrong with this trend, calling it "entry-level religion" that serves a good purpose.

There are countless more examples: the Evangelical Lutheran Church in America hopes to resurrect its beloved stop-action animated children's show, *Davey and Goliath*; a respected rabbi in Orlando teaches a well-attended course on "*Star Trek* and Judaism"; FM radio stations across the nation have adopted the "Contemporary Christian Music" format, making them sound—except for the songs' evangelical lyrics—like any other rock station; and there are more than forty-five million copies in print of Jerry Jenkins's and Tim LaHaye's Left Behind series of potboiler novels based on the book of Revelation (with a new LaHaye series coming about a Christian archaeologist who sounds a lot like the big-screen hero Indiana Jones). VeggieTales have sold twenty-five million videos and three million music CDs, with a full-length feature film coming next.

In fact, there appears to be no limit to this trend of appropriating and adapting popular culture in the service of religion, particularly for those who prefer their theology literal, "lite," and concrete. An evangelical group in Orlando hired a top-of-the line theme park designer to develop "The Holy Land Experience," a small, Bible-based tourist attraction near Universal Studios. Costumed characters, including Jesus (in season), roam a small recreation of first-century Jerusalem. The park, which describes itself as a "living Bible museum," claims its goal is to provide "a wholesome, family-oriented, educational and entertainment facility, where people can come and be encouraged, instructed and reinforced in their faith."

Is all this a good thing? Frankly, I'm of two minds on the intermingling of faith and entertainment. On the one hand, resorting to such lowest-common-denominator vehicles has the aroma of desperation on the part of organized religion. It is further evidence—if any more is needed—of the evaporating attention span of most Americans, and of the general dumbing down of serious discourse. Yet, undeniably, popular culture appears successful as a reference point in drawing in, on its level, many of the "unchurched," which accounts for my preparing this guide and for your reading it.

The debate over utilizing popular culture for evangelical purposes has been going on for a long time. During the Protestant Reformation five hundred years ago, Martin Luther was attacked for cribbing tavern ballad melodies for hymns. He is said to have retorted, "Why should the devil have all the good songs?" Terrence Lindvall, professor of communication at Pat Robertson's

Regent University in Virginia Beach, thinks this debate will continue. "The pendulum of faith in culture and faith opposing culture will continue to swing," he says. "At present, the parables and icons of the faith are colorfully animated for the entertainment of the churched and unchurched. Doctrine and dogma are viewed with suspicion—although *The Simpsons* and even Disney are not without their invisible worldviews, doctrines, and ethics. All media recommend how people should live, some even intentionally. They advise how we should view our families, work, sex, and now some are even promoting how we should understand religion. At the least, they will make it all entertaining."

Since I have always believed in truth in packaging, I need to tell you that most of the heavy lifting for this study guide was done by my coauthor, the Reverend Skip Parvin, pastor of Tuskawilla United Methodist Church, just outside Orlando. Skip has extensive experience in church youth work, writing, and analyzing popular culture from a religious and moral perspective. He knows what he is doing, which is why our editor at Westminster John Knox Press, David Dobson, chose him. This study guide is, to be sure, based on my book *The Gospel according to* The Simpsons: *The Spiritual Life of the World's Most Animated Family* and on an outline that I prepared. In addition, Skip and I consulted throughout the writing process. We have done our best to make this curriculum accessible to all religious groups and denominations. Scripture quotations are from both the Hebrew Bible and the New Testament. It goes without saying that *The Simpsons* episodes we have chosen can be appreciated by everyone, and I hope they will be.

Mark I. Pinsky

How to Use This Guide

Each chapter of this study guide is centered around one episode of *The Simpsons* (or, in some cases, *Family Guy*, *Futurama*, or *King of the Hill*) and is designed to stand alone as an individual session. Viewing the episode will require about thirty minutes, and we have provided enough in the way of activities and discussion questions to fill at least an additional hour.

While each session has been created with youth and young adults in mind, the sessions can be converted easily to work well with adults. The setting for using these sessions is left up to the leader, and there are several options. The leader can use them for a youth group program, a Sunday school class, a Bible study, or in any other educational setting. The sessions can be conducted wherever a television and VCR or DVD player are available. Despite the fact that each chapter is designed to stand alone, several of the sessions can be used in combination to form a *Simpsons* retreat or lock-in. The "Creation Care" session, based on *The Simpsons Movie* and *An Inconvenient Truth*, was especially designed for such a setting.

Always preview the episode you will be using at home before leading a session. Don't ever assume that you can remember everything about any episode. You will be surprised how much you can forget. These sessions are based on episodes that are commercially available at your local video store or media outlet. (The name of the compilation DVD that a particular episode can be

1

found on is identified in the next section of this guide.) In most areas of the United States and in many countries around the world, *Simpsons* episodes are shown several times a day, which makes it convenient to watch an episode without having to purchase or rent it. Just contact your local Fox television affiliate to find out when certain episodes will air. You can then schedule a time for your group to meet and watch the episode together.

This guide is designed to accompany the book *The Gospel according to* The Simpsons, *Bigger and Possibly Even Better! Edition*, by Mark I. Pinsky. Though it is not necessary, it will be helpful if each participant has a copy of that book. You as leader will certainly want to have a copy. The book can be found in your local bookstore or online.

Be mindful of the warning at the beginning of videotapes or DVDs that you rent or purchase. The rental or purchase of such videos gives you the right to show them in a home setting only, unless you purchase a license to show them elsewhere. Check with your pastor or director of education to see if your church or school already has such a license.

Episode Availability

Listed below are the DVD and VHS compilations where each episode can be found. Note that the more recent episodes are only available on DVD.

1. Dealing with Cults and Sects
The Simpsons Episode: "The Joy of Sect"
DVD: Season 9, Episode 13, Disc 2, No. 7

2. Spiritual Healing
The Simpsons Episode: "Faith Off"
DVD: Season 11, Episode 11, Disc 2, No. 6

3. What Is Our Mission?
The Simpsons Episode: "Missionary Impossible"
DVD: Season 11, Episode 15, Disc 3, No. 4

6. The Nature of God
Futurama Episode: "Godfellas"
DVD: Vol. 3, Disc 4, Episode 20

7. What about Hell?
Futurama Episode: "Hell Is Other Robots"
DVD: Vol. 1, Disc 2, Episode 9

8. Spiritual and Religious Tolerance
Family Guy Episode: "Holy Crap"
DVD: Vol. 1, Season 2, Disc 2

9. Talking about God
King of the Hill Episode: "Are You There, God? It's Me, Margaret Hill"
DVD: Season 6, Disc 2, Episode 12

The Simpsons

One

Dealing with Cults and Sects

Episode: "The Joy of Sect"

Synopsis: When Homer lets Bart skip school to meet the foot-ball team at the airport after a championship game, they encounter several people proselytizing for various spiritual move-ments and religions. Homer is intrigued by the Movementarians, who are offering a free weekend at a resort in order to present their beliefs. Homer and his family agree to attend the retreat. The recruiters work hard on Homer until he is finally converted. The Simpsons become part of the movement and move to an agricultural compound to live. When the premise of the move-ment is finally exposed as false, the Simpsons return to their regular lives.

Supplementary Reading: *The Gospel according to* The Simpsons, 2nd ed.: "Scientology and Tom Cruise," pp. 286–97; "The Cult," pp. 81–82

Old Testament Lesson: Ps. 40:4–5

Gospel Lesson: Matt. 24:4–8

Epistle Lesson: 1 John 4:1–4

Activity: Ask your group to name as many alternative or new spiritual movements as they can (this should take no more than five or ten minutes). Record these on a flip pad or whiteboard. Afterward, explain the definitions we are using here to define a

What Is the Difference between a Cult and a Sect?

The definition of the term "cult" has been broadened to the point that it has lost much of its original intention. The "politically correct" way to designate these groups is as "new" or "alternative" spiritual (or religious) movements (or communities). For our purposes here, a "cult" will be defined as a spiritual movement that centers around a charismatic leader who has great power and control over his or her followers. The group's practices and beliefs are usually highly unorthodox, occasionally extreme, and require the absolute commitment of those accepted for membership by the community. Most often these communities isolate themselves from conventional society physically, geographically, and through specific modes of dress and practice that set them apart from the larger culture. Avoid the definition forwarded by many evangelical Christians that basically states that any spiritual movement or religion other than orthodox Christianity is a "cult."

A sect is a small religious group that has broken off or moved in a more specific or different direction from a larger, well-established group. Most of the myriad denominations of the Christian church began as sects. In fact, Christianity was originally a sect of Judaism. While sects initially often have charismatic leaders, the disputes are usually about faith, practice, and differences in doctrinal understandings.

Generally speaking, if a "cult" survives the death of its charismatic leader and the community remains together, the group then is considered a "religion" in the widest sense of the definition. Most often, if a "sect" survives into a new generation, it sets itself apart from the larger religious body and becomes a new denomination or separate religion.

movement as a cult or sect. Help the group to work through the differences between the groups they have listed and where they would be placed according to the definitions above. This can be a bit tricky. Here are some general guidelines. According to the definition above, the following could be listed as cults: the People's Temple (Jim Jones, Jonestown), the Branch Davidians (David Koresh, Waco), Heaven's Gate (UFO group, San Diego) and the Manson Family (Charles Manson and his followers, Chatsworth, California). Even though Scientology and the Unification Church are treated as cults in this episode and have many of the attributes of cults, they have actually been classified as religions by the Internal Revenue Service. Groups such as the Church of Jesus Christ of Latter-day Saints (Mormons), Christian Scientists, and Jehovah's Witnesses are actually alternative forms of Christianity, although some mainstream and evangelical Christians continue to refer to them as cults or sects. Doing so is a way of marginalizing their members. At the time of its origin and for several centuries after, Christianity and associated groups were seen as sects or cults. Hinduism, Buddhism, Islam, Taoism, and other major religions, of course, are not "cults" (although some Christians want to see them that way). Here are some examples of "sects": the International Society for Krishna Consciousness (ISKCON) and Transcendental Meditation are sects of Hinduism. Opus Dei is a sect of Catholicism. And the Unitarian Universalist movement began as a sect of Christianity. Someone might bring up groups such as the Masons. The Masons are actually a fraternal organization with quasireligious rituals and practices. If you are not sure about a particular group, don't jump to conclusions in classifying it. You or the group can research it later.

Questions for Discussion: Prior to the discussion, have a member of the group read aloud each of the Scripture lessons.

- How is Homer originally recruited and swayed by the Movementarians? (Homer hears their original pitch about the planet "Blisstonia" while he and Bart are at the airport. He is tempted by the offer of a "free" weekend at a retreat center. Homer is a sucker for "free stuff.")

Scientology and Movementarianism

Clearly "Movementarianism" is meant to satirize Scientology. Scientology is a spiritual movement founded by popular science fiction writer L. Ron Hubbard in 1955. Scientologists believe that every person has the spiritual power to "clear" himself or herself of past hurtful and painful experiences through self-understanding and fulfillment through spiritual disciplines. Scientologists have often aggressively opposed attempts by the larger culture to denigrate, criticize, or satirize their movement (primarily through legions of high-priced lawyers). The movement is known publicly for its deep roots in the Hollywood community, and prominent Scientologists include Tom Cruise, John Travolta, and Kirstie Alley. It is interesting in this book to note that Nancy Cartwright, the voice of Bart Simpson, is a highly regarded Scientologist. In this episode, similarities between Movementarianism and Scientology include, but are not limited to: the light blue shirts, dark blue pants, and dark colored ties worn by the recruiters that reflect the dress of an elite group within Scientology known as the Sea Organization; like Movementarianism, Scientology offers free retreat weekends and an "orientation" film; the Movementarians have a "trillion year contract," similar to the billion year contract Scientologists sign binding them to the church when they become Sea Organization members; the judgment session to which Homer is subjected is similar to a Scientology training tool; and Scientology has weathered many conflicts over its standing as a "religion" and its tax-exempt status.

- What is Homer's initial motivation for joining the group? (Actually, in Homer's mind, things are reversed. He says, "These are some decent, generous people that I can take advantage of." Rather than being afraid that the group will manipulate and take advantage of him, he feels he can "work" them to meet his needs.)

• What do the Movementarians promise to the people they are recruiting? (They promise intergalactic transportation to a new and better life on the planet Blisstonia. One of the recruiters tells Homer, "When you surrender yourself to the Movementarians, you are guaranteed a perfect life of serenity and love, and loving serenity," but then quickly adds, "Nothing guaranteed.")

• Why do you think that people are attracted to these kinds of spiritual movements? (Usually people who join these movements are under some kind of financial, physical, emotional, or psychological distress. They are looking for a simple solution to their problems. They feel accepted for "who they are" and receive what seem to be unconditional love and attention from a community and its leader. They see this as an opportunity to "reinvent themselves" and make a fresh start in life and are willing to surrender their individual identity to the "larger good" of a community identity. Initially they often welcome their isolation from the larger world and are looking for a way to break away from their immediate situation with family, friends, or the community of which they are currently a part.)

• Homer faces what the Movementarians refer to as a "circle of judgment." What do you think the purpose of the circle is? How does Homer deal with it? (The circle of judgment, which is typical of cults, is designed to break down a person's self-esteem and individual identity. The group wants the person being judged to feel like a worthless failure [a state of mind to which the group provides an immediate remedy, of course]. Homer is basically guileless in his humility, understanding and accepting his personal weaknesses and shortcomings. A group can't break the self-esteem of a person who, for all intents and purposes, has no real self-esteem to begin with.)

• Lisa asks Homer, "Dad, do you think you might have been brainwashed?" What is she talking about? (One dangerous aspect of some alternative religious movements has been classified as "mind control." "Brainwashing" is an outmoded term for this process. Some groups use the combination of isolation, strict limitations in regard to behavior, absolute control of information, literal restrictions on what members are allowed to think, and manipulation of members both physically and emotionally to create complete dependence on the community and its leader. It is often difficult to break the psychological connection this practice creates in a movement's followers.)

- Does Jesus' warning to his disciples in Matthew 24:4–8 relate to the issue of cults? (Jesus warns his disciples that after he is gone many will say, "'I am the Messiah!' and they will lead many astray." He wants his followers to be extremely careful in regard to what they believe and whom they choose to follow. It is also clear that Jesus is warning them that other Christians may even try to manipulate them and undermine what they believe. He emphasizes that no matter what they experience in the world around them, they should continue to focus on his teachings and commandments until creation draws to an end.)

- What does the writer of 1 John 4:1–4 have to say about alternative spiritual movements? (The writer of 1 John offers practical advice for dealing with alternative forms of spirituality and belief. First, we should never accept or trust any spiritual claim without putting it to the test. The Holy Spirit will guide us in understanding what is authentic and what is false. This process will lead us to an understanding of what teachings we should accept and what teachings are unacceptable. Many contemporary scholars have suggested that when the writer of 1 John uses the phrase "the spirit of the antichrist," he is not actually talking about a person but any mindset or cultural movement that is opposed to Jesus Christ.)

- How do the Simpsons eventually break free from the Movementarians? (Marge sets up a clever demonstration in which she shows the children "hoverbikes"—bikes that supposedly fly. Then she shows them that the flying bikes are an illusion created by suspending the bikes in the air with fishing line. Even though the children wanted to believe that the bikes

Other Spiritual Movements Lampooned in This Episode

Krishna Consciousness. The International Society for Krishna Consciousness (ISKCON), also known as the "Hare Krishna" movement, is a religious sect of Hinduism founded in the United States in 1966 and based on Vedic scriptures. Groups of adherents engage in the joyful chanting of "Hare Krishna" (after the name of the Hindu god Krishna) and other mantras. In popular culture, devotees are stereotypically seen at airports with shaved heads and wearing saffron robes and tennis shoes while singing and dancing. They practice vegetarianism and celibacy.

Heaven's Gate. This American UFO cult was located primarily in San Diego and was led by Marshall Applewhite. The group was obsessed with the appearance of Comet Hale-Bopp in 1997. Applewhite was able to convince thirty-eight of his followers to commit suicide, which he claimed would make it possible for their souls to board a spaceship that they believed was hiding behind the comet.

The Unification Church. Followers of the Unification Church, founded by the Korean religious leader Sun Myung Moon, are often referred to disparagingly as "the Moonies." The beliefs of the Unification Church are based on Moon's book, *Divine Principle*, and combine teachings of the Bible with Asian beliefs and traditions. These beliefs include a single, all-powerful God, the idea that a literal kingdom of heaven can be created on earth, and the universal salvation of all human beings. Members also believe that Sun Myung Moon himself is the second coming of Jesus Christ. One of their most often satirized practices is the mass wedding, which has been performed by Moon on several occasions (Homer and Marge participate in a Movementarian mass wedding.)

could fly, in the end they knew that bikes don't actually fly. Homer and the family go through a similar process of realization when the spaceship that the leader of the Movementarians has been keeping secreted away in the barn proves to be an elaborate hoax. To a certain extent, the way they arrive at this conclusion reflects the advice found in the passage from 1 John.)

Prayer: God our Creator, help us to be patient and tolerant when dealing with other persons' spirituality. Rather than judging, help us to understand. Rather than rejecting, help us to reach out. Rather than arguing, help us to share. Rather than standing apart, help us find ways to appreciate one another and come together. Help each person to discover your great love and grace as you reveal yourself to us. Amen.

Something to Talk About: A great Web site for additional aspects of this discussion is found at http://www.religioustolerance.org/cults.htm.

Two

Spiritual Healing

Episode: "Faith Off"

Synopsis: When Homer visits his old college for homecoming, he gets together with his college buddies. He plans an elaborate prank, but, as always, the prank backfires and Homer ends up with a bucket glued on his head. Nothing will get it off, so the Simpson family ends up at a tent show revival featuring a faith healer named Brother Faith. During the service Brother Faith encourages Bart to pull the bucket from Homer's head. When the bucket comes loose in his hands, Bart is convinced that he "has the power" and decides to become a faith healer himself. When a miracle involving his friend Milhouse goes terribly wrong, Bart realizes that he should give up faith healing. Later, however, when Homer runs over Springfield's kicker with his homecoming float, the kicker's leg is hanging by a thread. When the doctor is unable to reattach the leg, Homer begs Bart to perform one more miracle. Once Bart has "healed" him, the kicker returns to the field with his leg taped on. In a bizarre turn of events the kick is good and the game is won.

Supplementary Reading: *The Gospel according to* The Simpsons, 2nd ed.: "Pentecostalism and Charismatic Worship," pp. 83–85

Old Testament Lessons: Jer. 17:13–14; Ps. 107:19–21

Gospel Lesson: Mark 5:22–34

Epistle Lesson: Jas. 5:13–16

Activity: On a whiteboard or flip chart write the following: "When I hear the words 'faith healing' I think of . . ." Give the members of the group about five minutes to write their responses. Encourage them to react spontaneously and offer impressions and memories rather than just a definition. When they are finished writing, ask them to share their responses. You might get a mixture of references to tent shows, faith healers, and TV evangelists. You might also get a few examples from popular culture, but you will likely have some members share personal experiences. Use what is shared here as a transition to more detailed discussions about the theology and practical aspects of spiritual healing.

Questions for Discussion: Prior to the discussion, have a member of the group read aloud each of the Scripture lessons.

- How do the Simpsons initially get involved with Brother Faith's revival and healing service? (After one of his silly pranks has backfired, Homer is stuck [literally] with a bucket glued to his head. The family tries every way possible to break the bucket loose, but it remains firmly attached. Homer has Bart drill two eyeholes in the bucket so he can see. Homer takes the family out for a drive, but he obviously can't see that well with a bucket on his head and ends up driving through a cornfield and into a ditch. When the family gets out of the car they realize that they have stumbled upon an old-fashioned tent show revival. Be sure to point out the serendipity of the Spirit involved here. The Simpsons didn't set out to attend a healing service, but were lead to one by the coincidence of circumstance.)

- What does Brother Faith preach? (Like most tent show evangelists he preaches faith. He even references John 2:11, which is the concluding verse of John's description of Jesus' first miracle—changing water into wine. Revival preachers often emphasize faith in their preaching. They maintain that one must have faith in order to be healed. That way, if they fail to heal a person, they can fall back on the excuse that the person being healed "didn't have enough faith.")

- Is Brother Faith a charlatan, or is he sincere? (Opinions will probably vary, but guide the group away from the generalization that Brother Faith is a fraud because "all faith healers are frauds." Brother Faith seems sincere. In his introduction, the announcer admonishes the crowd to give it up "for the healing love of Brother Faith." Brother Faith asks the crowd, "Do you want to be saved?" but does not preach fire and brimstone or threaten hell. He doesn't use guilt and negativity as a motivator and gives credit to the Holy Spirit: "Now let's hear it, for the Holy Spirit. No need to fear it, just revere it. He works in heaven. That's a 24/7!" When he lays hands on a person for healing he says, "The power of faith compels you—heal!" For reference, this line echoes a phrase often used in exorcisms— "The power of Christ compels you." Where Brother Faith gets off track is in giving Bart the impression that healing is a personal power rather than a gift of the Holy Spirit.)

- How does Bart come to believe that he has the power to heal? (Brother Faith actually asks for a "holy helper," "someone who believes." He calls Bart up and has him repeat "I have the power," and when he says it with conviction the bucket slips off of Homer's head. Brother Faith lifts Bart up to the crowd and says, "This child has . . . the power.")

- What's wrong with the idea that Bart "has the power"? (The power of spiritual healing is not "possessed" by any human being; it is the power of God's Holy Spirit working through us and our faith.)

- Does Bart actually believe he has the power at first? (No. He goes to speak privately with Brother Faith after the show and asks him, "How did you 'really' get the bucket off my Dad's head?" Brother Faith once again reinforces the idea that God gave Bart the "power" to remove the bucket. Bart replies that, given his attitude and behavior, he thought God would be more likely to "limit his power.")

- How does Bart respond when Brother Faith shares the testimony that when he was young he, too, was a "hell-raiser" like

Bart, but "changed his wicked ways." (Bart replies, "I think I'll go for the life of sin followed by a presto-change-o deathbed confession." This presents an opportunity for your group to discuss how they feel about the whole idea of the "deathbed confession.")

- How does Brother Faith counter Bart's argument? (Brother Faith admonishes Bart, "Why not spend your life helping people instead. Then you're also covered in case of sudden death." Bart is intrigued by this idea of "full coverage," of thinking of spiritual commitment like an insurance policy.)

- What finally convinces Bart that he does indeed "have the power"? (Bart is telling the story to the other kids when Ralph asks if Bart can heal him because he can't "breathe good." When Bart slaps Ralph and says, "Devil, begone," Ralph's milk money falls out of his nose. The kids see this as another "miracle," and Bart is convinced that it's true.)

- How does Lisa react to all this? (Always the skeptic, Lisa has a logical explanation for the "miracle of the bucket." She suggests that the bright lights on the stage heated the metal bucket and expanded it, making it easier to slip from Homer's head.)

- Why does Bart decide to start his own healing revival? (The Simpsons are in church when Reverend Lovejoy asks Bart if he's bored. Bart replies, "Church can be fun! No, really, it can be a crazy party with clouds and lasers and miracles. . . . A real preacher knows how to bring the Bible alive through music and dancing and Tae-Bo!")

- Should church services be "entertaining"? (The responses to this will likely include a range of personal opinions. Eventually the discussion should resolve with the idea that spirituality and entertainment can work together but there needs to be a balance and moderation.)

- What does the story of the woman who was healed in a crowd by touching Jesus' cloak (Mark 5:22–34) have to say about spiritual healing? (First, this story is embedded in another famous story about the healing of Jairus's daughter. If you want to read further, the group can discuss the resolution of that story as well. One of the most important points to make here is that Jesus never says, "I have healed you." Instead, he almost always tells the person healed, "Your faith has made you well." This is an important distinction. Spiritual healing works through our faith in conjunction with the power of the Holy Spirit.)

- What does James 5:13–16 suggest about spiritual healing? (This is James's advice for his and other Christian communities. He guides them into gathering together the community to pray and anoint those suffering with oil, which is the equivalent of the laying on of hands. He also directs them to sing songs of praise and to confess their sins. However, the most important

---

Healing Ministries and Mainline Churches

No longer are healing services found just in tent shows, television evangelism, and Pentecostal churches. Intentional healing ministries are becoming much more common in mainstream churches. Many Catholic, Protestant, and Jewish congregations are incorporating traditional healing services with the laying on of hands (and even anointing with oil) as a regular feature of their worship services and care-giving ministries. Traditionally, faith healing was thought to be in conflict with biomedical alternatives. These days it isn't that uncommon to see a surgeon praying with a patient before surgery. The Reverend Nancy J. Lane, an Episcopal priest from the Diocese of Central New York who has cerebral palsy, sums up this newly perceived need for transformation and healing: "People are hungry for healing in their lives, and we know that many turn to the latest trend in search of spirituality and healing. We need to teach people about healing and spread the word about God's healing work today. It may be the best evangelizing tool we have."

element of spiritual healing for James is the power of prayer. James says, "The prayer of faith will save the sick" and "The prayer of the righteous is powerful and effective.")

- What finally convinces Bart that he doesn't "have the power" and is not a healer? (A "miracle" performed by Bart on Milhouse goes horribly wrong. Milhouse thinks his vision has been "healed" by Bart and that he no longer needs glasses. He proceeds to walk out into the middle of the street and a van flattens him, putting him in the hospital. Bart realizes that his egotism has led to his friend's suffering. He begins to understand that human beings cannot possess the power to heal. Only God heals through God's Holy Spirit.)

- How does Bart's healing of the field goal kicker differ from his other attempts to heal people? (There are three significant differences. First, Bart approaches the healing of Lubchenko's leg with humility. He realizes that whatever happens will not happen because he has a special gift or power. Second, Bart prays for God's help when he lays his hands on Lubchenko's leg just as the writer of James suggests. Third, the prayer is heartfelt, sincere, and lifts up others beside himself. He prays not just for himself but for Lubchenko and Homer as well.)

Prayer: God of hope and promise, we know that your Spirit brings healing and peace to our broken and chaotic lives. We understand how much you love us and that you want the best for us. Even when we are in serious trouble, challenged by pain and suffering, we do not need to be afraid, but to trust you. We know that you will enter into our experience, heal our brokenness, and make us whole.

Something to Talk About: There are two movies that would be perfect to pair with this episode of *The Simpsons* if you wanted to expand this session into a retreat format.

- *Leap of Faith* (1992, 108 minutes, PG-13). Steve Martin, Debra Winger, Liam Neeson, Lolita Davidovich, and Lukas Haas star in this exploration of the complex web of theological and personal issues surrounding spiritual healing. Steve Martin plays Jonas Nightengale, a big league con man who has chosen tent show evangelism as a way to make money. He usually only works big cities, but when one of his trucks breaks down outside Rustwater, a small town in Kansas, he decides to make the best of it. The area has been stricken by drought, and the people have little more than what's needed to make ends meet. When an actual healing miracle occurs at one of his shows, Jonas is forced not only to reevaluate the way he makes a living but his life and relationships as well. The movie ends with a poignant example of the serendipity of God's grace and Spirit.

- *Marjoe* (1972, 88 minutes, PG). This movie, remastered and rereleased in 2006, won the Academy Award in 1973 for best documentary. It actually goes behind the scenes to expose the manipulative techniques and outright fraud that some tent show evangelists use to fleece the flock. When Marjoe was three years old, his parents introduced him to the tent show circuit as the world's youngest ordained evangelist, preacher, and faith healer. Just after Marjoe turned 16, his father abandoned the family and absconded with the nearly $3 million the family had accumulated while on tour. Disillusioned, Marjoe left home. In his early twenties and with scarce resources, however, he decided to go back on the tent show circuit with a captivating, high-budget stage show and a preaching style he patterned after Mick Jagger. The show was a huge success. In the early seventies Marjoe had a crisis of conscience about the unethical practices he was using to separate the crowds from their cash. Under the guise of filming an informative documentary, Marjoe gave the filmmakers unlimited "behind the scenes" access and instructed them to expose the fraudulent practices that he and some other tent show healers and evangelists used. The result is some of the most stunning footage of spiritual manipulation and greed ever filmed. You and your group will be amazed by this shocking look at fraudulent healers and evangelists.

Three

What Is Our Mission?

Episode: "Missionary Impossible"

Synopsis: When Homer anonymously donates $10,000 to PBS in order to save his favorite show, but with no intention of following through on his pledge, he is hunted down by an angry PBS mob demanding that he "pay up." Homer winds up hiding in the First Church of Springfield, and he makes a deal with Reverend Lovejoy to help him escape the angry mob. Lovejoy sends Homer on the next plane to become a missionary on a small island in the South Pacific. Homer knows next to nothing about Christianity, the Bible, or missionary work in general, but he decides that the best thing for the people of the island is to have them build a casino. As is typical of Homer's schemes, the casino creates horrible problems for the culture of the island. Homer then tries to make things right by building a church, but this project, of course, ends in disaster as well.

Supplementary Reading: *The Gospel according to* The Simpsons, 2nd. ed.: "The Church and the Preacher," pp. 91–92 (and other references on pp. 19 and 121)

Old Testament Lessons: 1 Chron. 16:23–24; Isa. 49:5–6

New Testament Lesson: Matt. 28:19–20

Epistle Lesson: Acts 1:8

Activity: Write the following phrase on a whiteboard or flip pad: "My most moving moment while participating in a local service mission or mission trip was . . ." It is likely that at least some members of your group will have been on short-term mission trips either overseas or in the United States. These experiences often create deeply gratifying memories for participants. Have members of the group share these memories with each other. You also might want to ask them to discuss significant people they may have met on those trips and what they learned from them.

Another idea you might consider is bringing a missionary or someone who has extensive mission experience to your group meeting to participate in the discussion and answer questions.

Questions for Discussion: Prior to the discussion, have a member of the group read aloud each of the Scripture lessons.

- Why do you think Reverend Lovejoy decides to send Homer off as a missionary? (Obviously the church must be desperate for anyone to send to this mission field. Homer knows next to nothing about Christianity, the Bible, or missionary work in general. However, even though Homer protests that he doesn't even believe in "Jebus" [the mispronunciation is a running joke in the series], Homer then proceeds to pray desperately that "Jebus" get him out of the mess he's in. Missionary service is a specialized calling to service and requires significant dedication and preparation, neither of which Homer has.)

- What is the attitude of Craig and Amy, the departing missionaries? (They tell Homer to "forget everything he learned in missionary school," to which he replies, "Done." Then they explain, "We taught them some English and ridiculed away most of their beliefs. So you can take it from there." Later one of the islanders mentions that Craig and Amy gave them "the gift of shame." This represents a more nineteenth-century attitude toward missions. Amy and Craig clearly sought to Westernize the islanders rather than respecting their culture.)

- How does Marge react to Homer's missionary activities? (She is proud that he's showing "an interest in his fellow man." In response, Homer tells her, "I've got some civilization to spread like butter on the English muffin that is these people, with all their nooks and crannies" and begins referring to himself as "Humanitarian Homer Simpson.")

- What is Homer's first approach to working with the natives? (He makes a genuine effort to be a teacher. They want to learn about the Bible, but they cannot read, and Homer knows little that he can share. The islanders begin asking some probing questions, such as, "Why does God need to be worshiped" and "What is the 'right' religion?" Homer soon realizes that he is in over his head.)

- Why does Homer suggest building a casino? (Homer has the best of intentions, but the road to "Homer Hell" is always paved with good intentions. Homer thinks the island needs some "razzle-dazzle." He knows that casinos have revitalized the economies of communities back home—why wouldn't that work here? At first, even Marge is impressed. However, the negative influences of gambling begin to take their toll on the island paradise. One of the islanders observes, "Our island has not been this damaged since the A-bomb tests.")

- How does Homer respond to the crisis? (In order to "repent," Homer sets about leading the community in completing the chapel that Craig and Amy had started building to provide a place of worship for the islanders. Homer scares them into helping him by telling them that building the chapel will help them escape from the hellfire and brimstone to come. When they are finished Homer says, "I may not know much about God, but I have to say we built a pretty nice cage for him." The islanders question why they must attend church in order to avoid hell.)

- What does Matthew 28:19–20 have to say about missions? (This, of course, is the Great Commission, Jesus' direction to his followers before he ascends to heaven. The verse is less

Missionaries: Then and Now

When Europeans first colonized the New World, the indigenous people were often viewed as subhuman savages. Some priests even argued that they had no souls and were created by God to be slaves. Those who did not die of diseases such as smallpox were treated brutally and often slaughtered in a genocidal frenzy. A story is told of the Indian Chief Hatuey, who fled with his people from the invaders but was captured and sentenced to be burned alive. As "they were tying him to the stake a Franciscan friar urged him to take Jesus to his heart so that his soul might go to heaven, rather than descend into hell." Hatuey replied, "If heaven is where the Christians go, I would rather go to hell" (D. Stannard, *American Holocaust* [Oxford University Press, 1992]). This was not a good start in offering grace and love to a new people.

By the nineteenth century the goal of many missionaries was to Westernize the peoples they encountered. Their goal was not only to convert the people to Christianity but to convert them to Western dress, manners, language, and culture with little regard to their indigenous cultural heritage and the richness of their history and traditions.

Contemporary missionaries work to help the people they serve in their areas of most immediate need and to train them in skills that will help to sustain them in the future. The message the missionaries share is offered in the context of the culture, customs, and history of the people being served. As the great liberation theologian Gustavo Gutiérrez has said, "To be followers of Jesus requires that [we] walk with and be committed to the poor; when [we] do, [we] experience an encounter with the Lord who is simultaneously revealed and hidden in the faces of the poor" (Gustavo Gutiérrez, *We Drink from Our Own Wells* [Orbis Books, 2003]).

about "converting" and "saving" people than it is about model-
ing the life of discipleship through which people will establish
their own relationship with God. Jesus' commandments were
simple and straightforward: Love God above all else, love your
neighbor as yourself, and love one another as you have been
loved by Jesus. This demonstrates that outreach into the world
as a mission is more about sharing unconditional love and grace
rather than helping people "escape from hell.")

- What does Acts 1:8 add to our understanding of missions?
  (First, it's not about us but about the power of the Holy Spirit
  working through us. This is an important distinction. Second,
  Jesus directs us to be "witnesses." Outreach through missions
  is not so much about sharing a theological point of view as it is
  about bearing witness to the ways in which unconditional love
  has transformed our lives. Our hope is that once others see how
  spiritual transformation has taken place in our lives, they will
  begin a relationship with God that will transform theirs.)

- What is the Hebrew (Jewish or Old Testament) understanding
  of missions reflected in 1 Chronicles 16:23–24 and Isaiah
  49:5–6? (The Jewish people did not think of missions as "converting" Gentiles to Judaism. They saw their entire community
  of faith as an example of God's desire to reconcile all human
  beings to God. God states it this way through Isaiah: "I will give
  you as a light to the nations, that my salvation may reach to the
  end of the earth." So it is the witness of the entire community,
  "as a light to the nations," that matters most to God's salvation
  reaching "to the end of the earth.")

- Ask if anyone in your group has been on a mission trip to a
  Native American reservation. Do you see parallels between the
  desperate poverty there and the decisions Native American
  communities have made to become involved in casino gambling? Do you think that this episode of *The Simpsons* can call
  our attention to this situation? What corrupting or negative
  influences does casino gambling potentially bring with it? (It's
  clear that the writers of this *Simpsons* episode wanted to make

the comparison between casinos on Native American land and Homer's situation in Microatia. The big difference is that the people of Microatia seem to have a much better life and less poverty because they are a self-sustaining culture. In addition to the problem of compulsive gambling [or gambling addiction], other problems accompanying the institution of casino gambling will often include a rise in bankruptcies, foreclosures, family violence, crime [violent crime as well as theft or robbery], divorce, alcoholism, and suicide.)

- Have you ever experienced participants on a mission trip who didn't seem sincere about what they were doing? Did you experience participants who stereotyped or exhibited inappropriate attitudes toward the persons being served? (This will obviously be a matter of personal experience; however, stereotyping and holding inappropriate attitudes toward the people being served will occasionally create tension in mission situations. Often this will result from a lack of understanding [or complete ignorance] about the culture and customs of the mission setting. Occasionally people will approach mission trips as a way to fill obligations for community service hours or to be able to list the mission trip on their resumes or college applications. Having a "heart" for missions is an essential element of serving others in these situations.)

Prayer: To end the session, pray together the Prayer of St. Francis. This prayer presents a wonderful summation of the ways we can best share our faith with others:

> Lord, make me an instrument of Thy peace;
> Where there is hatred, let me sow love;
> Where there is injury, pardon;
> Where there is doubt, faith;
> Where there is despair, hope;
> Where there is darkness, light;
> And where there is sadness, joy.
> O Divine Master,

Grant that I may not so much seek to be consoled as to
   console;
To be understood, as to understand;
To be loved, as to love;
For it is in giving that we receive,
It is in pardoning that we are pardoned,
And it is in dying that we are born to Eternal Life.
Amen.

Something to Talk About: Several excellent movies deal with the issues and attitudes surrounding missionary outreach and would be good to use if you were to expand this session to a retreat format.

- *At Play in the Fields of the Lord* **(1991, 189 minutes, R).** Fundamentalist missionaries Martin and Hazel Quarrier (Aidan Quinn and Kathy Bates) are sent to the jungles of South America to convert an indigenous tribe. The indigenous people terrify Hazel, while her husband Martin is fascinated by them, especially by their primitive power. When an American pilot "goes native" and joins the tribe (Tom Berenger), a clash of cultures ensues.

- *The Mission* **(1986, 126 minutes, PG).** Father Gabriel (Jeremy Irons) has come to the mountains as a missionary, to serve the people and offer them Christianity. Rodrigo Mendoza (Robert De Niro) is a military man and a slave trader who has murdered his brother and believes that his penance is to give up his former life and become a missionary under Father Gabriel's guidance. Eventually, Mendoza takes his vows to become a priest. When Spain and the Catholic Church cede the mountains to Portugal, the mountain people are placed in danger of being captured and traded as slaves by the Portuguese. Gabriel is a man of peace and urges nonviolence and diplomacy with the new imperialistic regime. Mendoza, well aware of what the slave traders will do to the people, defies his vows and organizes the natives to defend themselves from the coming onslaught.

The Mission has been considered by many to be a metaphorical look at the tensions created by liberation theology.

- *Hawaii* **(1966, 162 minutes, MPAA approved—contains some nudity and violence).** Based on a novel by James Michener and featuring a screenplay by Dalton Trumbo, *Hawaii* is a classic film dealing with the clash between cultures when Western missionaries first arrive in the Hawaiian islands.

- *End of the Spear* **(2005, 108 minutes, PG-13).** This film is based on the true story of a group of Christian missionaries who came to Ecuador to reach out to an indigenous people called the Wadani. The Wadani people are an extremely violent tribe who place a strong cultural emphasis on revenge killing. Five of the male missionaries are murdered with spears because the Wadani fear all outsiders are cannibals. Instead of leaving, the wives and children of the slain men join the Wadani village to teach love and forgiveness by their example. *End of the Spear* is a deeply moving story of how the power of grace can transcend any cultural divide.

- *Volunteers* **(1985, 107 minutes, R).** In this early effort by Tom Hanks, his character, Lawrence Whatley Bourne III, a spoiled rich boy, finds himself in a similar situation to Homer's. To escape gangsters who want to do him in for failure to pay a huge gambling debt, Lawrence cons his way onto a Peace Corps flight to Southeast Asia. Once there, his assignment is to lead the natives and other volunteers in building a bridge. Behind the scenes, the U.S. Army, a local communist guerilla force, and a powerful drug lord are contesting the bridge. The volunteers band together with the natives to "do the right thing." *Volunteers* would provide a bit of comic relief in the midst of the other intensely serious movies recommended here.

- *Black Robe* **(1991, 101 minutes, R).** Set in 1634, this film features Father Laforgue (Lothaire Bluteau), a French Jesuit missionary, who sets out on a 1,500-mile trek into the Canadian wilderness (in present-day Quebec) in order to reestablish a remote mission and convert the Huron people. When Father Laforgue finally reaches the mission outpost, he finds one missionary dead, the other dying, and the Huron people devastated by an epidemic of scarlet fever. Laforgue baptizes all of the natives, but an epilogue describes the nearly immediate fall of the Hurons when the Iroquois conquer them.

Some helpful books for exploring the ideas behind missions include:

Teaching Mission in a Global Context by Patricia Lloyd-Sidle and Bonnie Sue Lewis (Westminster John Knox Press, 2001)

Global Good News: Mission in a New Context by Howard A. Snyder (Abingdon Press, 2001)

Mission: An Essential Guide by Carlos Cardoza-Orlandi (Abingdon Press, 1999)

Ready-to-Go Devotions for Mission and Service by Mark Ray (Abingdon Press, 2008)

Four

Creation Care: A Green Retreat Based on *The Simpsons Movie* and *An Inconvenient Truth*

Scripture Lesson: Gen. 1:1, 31a

Commentary: This lesson combines the first verse of Genesis with God's proclamation at the end of the initial process of creation. God, being eternal, has selected a moment in time to bring creation into being. God is the "first cause" of the creative process by which the universe and everything in it ("the heavens and the earth") comes to exist. Once God has set creation into motion, God proclaims that "it was very good." God's attitude toward creation is one of original blessing; all that is part of the process of creation is "very good," and God's ultimate desire is for creation to continue to be as good as it was when it was begun.

Scripture Lesson: Gen. 2:15

Commentary: In Hebrew the fundamental meaning of the word translated "to till" or "to tend" (*'abad*) is "to work" or "to serve." The Hebrew word that is translated "keep it" (*shamar*) means to "take care of," "preserve," or "protect." God's intention is not that human beings have dominion over creation to use it any way we choose. This verse demonstrates that God does not want human beings to degrade, deplete, or destroy that creation. Human beings are intended to serve creation by caring for it, preserving it, and protecting it. God's mandate here is clear.

Scripture Lesson: Num. 35:33–34

Commentary: On the surface these verses seem to be only about the pollution of the land by blood (blood guilt). Murder (unjustified and inappropriate killing) defiles, debases, and corrupts the land with the blood of its victims. However, pollution by blood is only an extreme example of the many ways that the Israelites could defile and debase the land. The covenant between Israel and God in regard to the land is clear. It is a gift, a sign of God's grace. It is to be valued, cared for, nurtured, and preserved. To pollute the land in any way is anathema to God.

Scripture Lesson: Job 12:7–10

Commentary: These verses are not about Job's being some kind of "Dr. Doolittle" wandering around and having conversations with animals, birds, plants, and fish. Rather, they are part of a defense that Job makes to his faithless and disloyal friends who insist that God has abandoned him and, even worse, is punishing him. Job responds with a long discourse in which he argues that even when God seems silent, God can be perceived in the intricacies of the natural world God has created. The animals, birds, plants, and fish teach us all we need to know about God's relationship with God's creation. Job's argument here is that no person who carefully observes the complex interwoven details of creation could possibly miss the fact that the hand of God is present in all that he or she sees. How can Job's friends, confronted with the wonders of creation, not understand that "the life of every living thing and the breath of every human being" is the only evidence we need to convince us that God is not only present but powerfully moving in the world around us?

Scripture Lesson: Isa. 24:4–6

Commentary: These verses are part of a prophecy of catastrophe known as "Isaiah's Apocalypse." Creation "dries up and withers" because "the earth lies polluted under its inhabitants." The cause of this calamity is Israel's transgression of laws, violation of statutes, and breaking of its covenant with God regarding the land.

As with the passage from Numbers 35:33–34, the primary form of pollution is "blood guilt." But the shedding of innocent blood isn't the only reason the earth languishes. The Israelites have committed multiple transgressions against the land in violation of their covenant with God to treat the land as a sacred gift. In this case the curse that "devours the earth" is a direct consequence of the people's refusal to take responsibility for their actions and care for the land.

Scripture Lesson: Jer. 2:7

Commentary: When the Israelites settled in the promised land, their first attitude should have been one of deep gratitude. But rather than thanking God for the land, they actually ignored God. In verse 8, God says through Jeremiah that the priests did not ask the most important question—"Where is the Lord in all this?" Rather, they "defiled" God's land and made God's heritage "an abomination." In Jeremiah 1:10 God commissions Jeremiah not only to "to pluck up and pull down, to destroy and overthrow," but also "to build and to plant."

Scripture Lesson: Jer. 12:4

Commentary: The most important aspect of this verse is the personification of the land itself. Jeremiah has the people of Israel think about the land in personal terms. The land is "mourning," and it is as if the grass is "withering away" in sorrow. The animals and birds (necessary for the Israelites' survival) are "swept away" because the people do not care to preserve them and believe that God "is blind" to what they are doing. Jeremiah reminds the Israelites that nothing could be further from the truth.

Scripture Lesson: Rom. 1:19–22

Commentary: This New Testament passage could be paired with Job 12:7–10, as both passages have the same theme. It also echoes the previous verse from Jeremiah. "What can be known about God" should be plain to us in that every aspect of creation demonstrates the power and divinity of God. Even though it is "invisible," it can be clearly perceived by those who are willing to acknowledge it. The people should be grateful for what God has provided, but they ignore the presence of God in creation and have become "futile in their thinking," and their "senseless minds" have become darkened. "Claiming to be wise," they instead have become fools.

Scripture Lessons: John 1:3–5 and Col. 1:15–20

Commentary: These two passages testify to the same understanding of the nature of creation. Christians believe that creation itself is christocentric, or "Christ centered." The person of God revealed in Jesus of Nazareth was, and is, part of God through all eternity. God has no beginning and no end, so neither does the nature of God revealed in Jesus have a beginning or an end. The Gospel of John begins by stating the primacy of Christ in the creation of all things. The passage from Colossians takes this one step further. Not only were all things "created through him and for him," it is in Christ that "all things hold together." Paul makes an even more dramatic claim by suggesting that God's intention is to eventually redeem all of creation through Jesus, because in Jesus "God was pleased to reconcile to himself all things, whether on earth or in heaven, by making peace through the blood of his cross." This is one of Paul's most radical assertions.

Scripture Lesson: Rom. 8:19–22

Commentary: The eighth chapter of Romans is one of the most often quoted sections of Paul's letters. Here, in verses 19–20, much like in Jeremiah 12:4, Paul personifies creation, suggesting that creation "waits with eager longing" for the coming of Christ, that it might be "set free from its bondage to decay." Like a woman giving birth to a baby, creation "has been groaning in labor pains until now" in anticipation of new birth, redemption, and freedom from the "futility" to which it has been subjected. Paul links the redemption of human beings to the redemption of creation itself.

The Simpsons Movie (2007, 87 minutes, PG-13)

Synopsis: The movie begins with the band Green Day in concert on a stage sitting atop a barge floating in Lake Springfield. When the band members pause to give an appeal for the environment, the people of Springfield start pummeling them with whatever they can find to throw. While this is happening, the hull of the barge is dissolved by the pollution in Lake Springfield, drowning the band. At a memorial for the group, Grampa Simpson is slain by the Spirit, with a vision of environmental doom for the city. Always the social activist, Lisa begins a campaign to save Lake Springfield from pollution that includes a presentation entitled, "An Irritating Truth." While canvassing the neighborhood, Lisa meets a boy named Colin, an ecologically conscious Irish musician, and she comes to believe that Colin is her soul mate. Meanwhile, Homer saves a pig from being slaughtered and makes him his pet, naming him "Spider Pig." Homer's new pet produces an abundance of "waste products" that Homer stores in a silo. When the silo is full, Marge insists that Homer dispose of the contents in an environmentally sensitive way; however, Homer dumps the waste into Lake Springfield, creating an ecological disaster (not to mention a mutant squirrel with a thousand eyes). An agent from the Environmental Protection Agency named Cargill convinces President Schwarzenegger to seal off the toxic town of Springfield in a glass dome so that there will be no possibility of the pollution contaminating the rest of the country. Disgraced, the Simpson family leaves town and heads for exile in Alaska. When Marge has a crisis of conscience and takes the rest of the family back to Springfield to help find a solution to the town's problem, Homer is faced with an overwhelming life decision. Does he live out his life in backwoods seclusion or return to the friends and family he loves? As always, Homer ends up doing the right thing, and he and Bart heroically save Springfield.

A partial transcript (in process) of *The Simpsons Movie* is available at the Simpson Crazy Web site: http://www.simpsoncrazy .com/scripts.php.

An Inconvenient Truth (2006, 100 minutes, PG)

Synopsis: Former Vice President Al Gore's personal history and commitment to reversing the effects of global climate change are the subjects of this fascinating film, which won the Oscar in 2007 for Best Feature Documentary. A longtime environmental crusader, Gore presents the science and statistics supporting global warming in a straightforward and compelling style infused with his personal charm and humor. Gore presents the facts as he sees them and challenges his audiences to draw their own conclusions. Gore's message is unambiguous: "It is now clear that we face a deepening global climate crisis that requires us to act boldly, quickly, and wisely." Gore and the United Nations' Intergovernmental Panel on Climate Change shared the 2007 Nobel Peace Prize for their work to promote worldwide awareness of the challenge presented by global climate change.

A complete transcript of *An Inconvenient Truth*, including all of Al Gore's presentation slides, is available at the Politics Blog: http://forumpolitics.com/blogs/2007/03/17/an-inconvient-truth -transcript.

Questions for Discussion: *The Simpsons Movie*

- The movie begins with an Itchy and Scratchy cartoon that has Scratchy landing on the moon only to find Itchy already there. In the background is the earth as seen from the surface of the moon. Do you think that the Simpsons crew wanted us to think about how small and fragile the "big blue marble" appears from space in relation to the universe? (Al Gore starts his presentation on global climate change by showing actual pictures of Earth taken from space to achieve this effect. *The Simpsons* crew has managed to slip the image in by beginning with this Itchy and Scratchy cartoon.)

- All of Springfield has turned out for a Green Day concert that is performed from a stage barge on Lake Springfield. When Green Day stops after three and a half hours to say something

Green Candied Popcorn

4 quarts popped corn   1/2 cup light corn syrup

1 1/2 cups sugar   2 tablespoons butter

1/2 teaspoon salt   1/4 teaspoon vanilla

Green food coloring (about 1/8 teaspoon Wilton paste color in kelly green is suggested)

1/4 teaspoon cream of tartar (optional, but does make mixture slightly more creamy)

In a heavy saucepan on medium heat, melt butter. Add sugar, corn syrup, cream of tartar, and salt. Increase temperature to medium high and bring mixture to a boil, stirring constantly to dissolve sugar. Once mixture boils, add in food coloring and stop stirring. Boil for 5 minutes (do not stir). Mixture should be about 250–260 degrees. Remove from heat and carefully stir in vanilla and baking soda. Working quickly and while mixture is foamy, pour mixture over popped corn and stir gently to coat popcorn. Place popcorn in a large roaster or rimmed baking sheet lined with parchment paper or sprayed with cooking spray and bake at 200 degrees for 1 hour, stirring every 15 minutes.

Adjust the recipe to the size of your group. This snack is relatively easy to mass produce. Enjoy it with any of the "green" movies highlighted in this chapter!

(Recipe used by permission of www.skiptomylou.org.)

about environmental concern, the people begin throwing things at the band. Do you think people are tired of celebrities promoting causes? Or does the celebrity promotion of a cause make the cause more attractive or "glamorous" to his or her fans? (Opinions will vary. While some celebrities are sincere in using their social status to promote causes, others seem to do it as much or more to promote themselves.)

- At a memorial service for Green Day at the First Church of Springfield, a beam of light shines on Grampa Simpson and he brings a vision of environmental doom for Springfield. Some of what he says is in symbolic language, and some of the rest is incomprehensible. How do you feel about this caricature of charismatic worship? (Some people will be offended by it. [Some people are offended by *The Simpsons* in general]. Others will find it funny. But it imbues what is about to happen with spiritual significance. The Simpsons are in church [as they often are] participating in the memorial service when Grampa is struck by "the light of the Spirit" to testify. It is a common theme in *Simpsons'* episodes to instill what is happening with spiritual significance.)

- In the car on the way home, when the rest of the family just seems to want to get to the waffle restaurant, Marge says, "What is the point of going to church every Sunday when if someone we love has a genuine religious experience we ignore it?" Do you think that "genuine religious experience" is often ignored or looked upon with skepticism by our culture? (Again, opinions will vary. People have a tendency to be afraid of something that they don't completely understand, and religious experiences often fall into this category. They can often make us uncomfortable by calling into question our own spiritual experiences or the lack thereof.)

- When Milhouse insists that he is "passionate about the planet" in order to convince Lisa to canvass him, the bully Nelson Muntz appears behind him and threatens to punch him in the stomach if he doesn't say, "Global warming is a myth!" When Milhouse quickly cries out, "It's a myth! Further study is needed!" Nelson punches him in the stomach anyway for "selling out his beliefs." Do you think people are swayed by peer pressure (adults as well as youth) when it comes to important issues of social concern? (Many people prefer to "go along to get along" in order to avoid being in the minority when it comes to family and friends. Some people assume that "all Democrats think this way" or "all Republicans think that way" when it is simply not the case. There are a number of people who refuse to be intimidated by others and stick to their beliefs even when they are different from those held by others.)

- While canvassing for the environment Lisa meets Colin, an Irish boy who has just moved to Springfield and is canvassing as well. Lisa is immediately smitten. Is it easier to hold a controversial opinion when someone you love stands beside you? Do you ever have conflicts with friends or family about controversial issues? (It's always easier to be in the minority when someone you love believes in you and is passionate about the same thing; however, this is often not the case. Have the group share stories about relationships with friends or family members who hold different political or social views.)

- While Bart is fishing with Flanders, Lisa witnesses toxic waste being dumped into Lake Springfield. She decides to have a symposium (which she entitles "An Irritating Truth"). Have you ever been moved to do something in response to a social injustice through a personal experience?

- Lisa's symposium actually motivates the town to clean up Lake Springfield, and the entire community works together to accomplish the goal. Are such projects taking place in your area? Is your community of faith involved? Have you participated in them? If not, what do you think would motivate the people of your area to act together to solve a problem that threatens your community?

- When Homer's pet pig produces enough waste to fill a silo in the backyard, Marge commissions Homer to "dispose of that waste properly." Homer, of course, dumps the waste into Lake Springfield. Why does Homer do this when he knows his actions could have a significant negative impact? (The line at the toxic waste disposal center is long and it looks like Homer will have to spend the better part of the day there. When he gets a call from a friend telling him that the donut store is giving out free donuts, Homer quickly dumps the waste into Lake Springfield. It is more convenient than disposing of the waste properly and allows Homer to get on to his more selfish pursuits. We simply have to look at the litter on the sides of our roads to realize that many people still operate from this mentality. It's simpler to do the wrong thing than to take time to do the right thing.)

- Homer's silo of waste tips the scales in Lake Springfield, making it completely toxic. The Environmental Protection Agency (EPA) concludes that the "pollution in Springfield has reached crisis levels." The EPA presents the president with "five unthinkable options," and the president elects to place a glass dome over Springfield. Despite the fact that this is impossible, what does it say about the way we sometimes approach problems that have reached crisis proportions? (Rather than getting to the root of the problem, stopping the toxic dumping, and cleaning up Lake Springfield, the government seals off the town so that it won't affect the rest of the nation. This does not solve the problem but is another way of denying it and keeping it hidden.)

- As the dome is lowered over the town, the people stream out of the First Church of Springfield and Moe's Bar (which just happen to be neighbors). The congregants run into the bar and the bar patrons rush into the church. What point is being made here? (Some people are only motivated to seek God in a time of crisis, seeing prayer and religious experience as a "last resort." Other people who have been part of a spiritual community might lose hope, fall into despair, and end up at a bar.)

- When it is revealed that Homer's dumping of the pig waste was the event that led to the town's being sealed off, Marge accuses him of being the one who "single-handedly killed this town," and Lisa accuses Homer of being a monster. The town forms an angry mob to bring Homer to justice (albeit vigilante justice). Is this fair to Homer? (No it isn't. Homer's dumping of the silo was just the last act in a series of acts that led to Lake Springfield's becoming completely toxic. The townspeople are scapegoating Homer for a problem that they all had a part in creating. It is often easier to blame one person or group for a crisis rather than to accept responsibility collectively.)

- Maggie discovers that the sinkhole in her sandbox is a passage to the outside. The Simpsons use it to escape the mob and get out of Springfield, becoming fugitives from the EPA. They decide to head for Alaska in order to get a fresh start. They find an idyllic setting on a lake and become survivalists. Is this a solution to their problems? (There is a movement in this country to escape to secluded rural areas in order to leave behind the problems created by our technologically based culture. While this might be a good choice for some, it reflects an attitude of surrender—the problems can't be resolved, so we will run from them. Escaping from a problem is not the same as solving it.)

- The EPA decides to destroy Springfield in order to create a "new Grand Canyon." Homer's family resolves to return home to rescue the town they love. Why does Homer stay behind? (Homer, like many people, is attracted to the easiest alternative when faced with a problem. He likes his life in Alaska and doesn't want to leave it. In the end, however, Homer decides to do the right thing.)

- What finally convinces Homer to return to be with his family and save Springfield? (Homer meets an Inuit shaman. [The Inuit are an indigenous Alaskan people. A shaman is a holy person who serves as a guide between the physical world and the spiritual world for a given group of tribal people.] The shaman guides Homer to discover his hidden spiritual truth. In a vision he discovers, "Other people are just as important as me. Without them, I'm nothing." In order to save himself he must save others, or in this case, Springfield.)

- As Springfield waits for the bomb to destroy the town, the camera pans to the sign outside the First Church of Springfield, which reads, "We told you so." What does this reflect about the way that some communities of faith view the world? (Some communities of faith have concluded that humanity is so corrupt that we are irredeemable. The only solution they see is for God to bring an end to creation. They warn of the imminent end of the world.)

- What is the result of Homer and Bart's heroic act to risk their lives in order to blow up the dome? (A consistent theme in *The Simpsons* is grace and redemption. Homer or Bart almost always does something incredibly stupid that causes horrible consequences. Through a process of self-discovery, they are led to do the right thing. As a result, they receive grace and forgiveness, which leads to their redemption.)

Questions for Discussion: *An Inconvenient Truth*

- Before showing the movie, have a brief discussion (15–20 minutes) about the ways members of the group think about global warming and climate change. What have they heard? What do they know? What do they believe? Have they been motivated to change their lifestyles? (You will probably get a wide range of opinions, ranging from deep concern to suggestions that the idea of climate change is a hoax. You might even have a few who say, "I've heard about it, but I haven't paid much attention to it.")

- After the movie ends and before you lead the group in discussing the details, ask, "How did this movie make you feel?" Did it change your way of looking at or perceiving the issue? Is Al Gore's argument convincing? Did Al Gore's style of presentation contribute to your willingness to listen to what he had to say? (This, of course, will be personal opinion; however, many people have found that the film has changed their attitudes toward the idea of climate change. Others may not have realized the depth of the dilemma. Some people may still insist that it is some kind of fabrication or conspiracy. Be patient and open-minded with all points of view.)

- Do you agree that the images of the earth taken from space have what Al Gore calls a "magical quality"? Do pictures like these of the earth make you think about creation in a different way?

(Pictures of the earth from space inspire a sense of how small and fragile our world is in relation to the rest of the universe. They also support the idea that we are all crew members on "Spaceship Earth," a term popularized by Buckminster Fuller [one of the earliest "whole earth" environmentalists], who published a popular book in 1963 with the title *Operating Manual for Spaceship Earth*. Many scholars believe that Fuller got the idea for the concept of Spaceship Earth from an even earlier proponent of whole earth environmentalism, Henry George, who said in *Progress and Poverty* [1879], "It is a well-provisioned ship, this on which we sail through space. If the bread and beef above decks seem to grow scarce, we but open a hatch and there is a new supply, of which before we never dreamed. And very great command over the services of others comes to those who as the hatches are opened are permitted to say, 'This is mine!' ")

- Al Gore begins his presentation with this quote from conventional wisdom: "What gets us into trouble is not what you don't know, but what you think you know that just ain't so." Do you agree that this kind of thinking is a problem? What are some examples from history of this kind of thinking? (It is close-minded to hold a position as true and not allow the ideas and discoveries of others to influence the way we think. Gore gives one example from his early education, a teacher who declared the idea that the continents once fit together as "ridiculous." Others would include the ideas that the earth is flat, that it is the center of the universe, and that it does not revolve around the sun.)

- Do you or somebody you know hold the assumption that the planet is so big that humans cannot possibly have any lasting, harmful impact on its environment? What do you think? (It seems to be obvious that, as part of the earth's ecosystem, human beings can have significant and lasting effects on the Earth's environment. The Scriptures, from Genesis 2:15, to Numbers 35:33–34, to Isaiah 24:4–6, to Jeremiah 2:7, stress the symbiotic relationship that human beings have with the environment. Each of these passages points to the lasting consequences that human behavior can have on the earth.)

- Which of the effects to the earth that Gore documents is of most concern or shocks you the most? (Gore points to the loss of glaciers, changes in mountains effecting watersheds, changes in the Arctic and Antarctica, the rise in ocean levels, loss of arable land, and intensified storm cycles, among others.)

- Gore makes the case that global climate change is both a moral issue (the difference between right and wrong) and an ethical issue (concern for the greatest good for the greatest number of people). As a person of faith, do you agree? (Members of the group may vary in their opinions. Some may not want to see it as an issue of absolute morality, but it's hard to dispute that this is a matter of grave ethical concern.)

- Do you feel that global climate change is a spiritual issue? (Having read the Scriptures provided with this guide, it would be difficult to defend a position that we should not see our relationship to the environment as a spiritual priority.)

- Gore talks about the attitudes of people shifting from denial (this isn't really happening) to despair (it's inevitable; we can't do anything to change it). How do we deal with despair? (As Christians we can never give in to despair. Despair is a loss of hope, and hope is a cornerstone of any spiritual commitment. Not only should we not lose hope, but we need to be a source of hope for others.)

- Has this film changed your outlook toward the relationship between spirituality and concern for the environment?

- Obviously, these two films take radically different strategies in calling attention to concern for the environment. Do you think one is more effective than the other? (Although Gore injects humor into his presentation, most of it is deadly serious. The humor and satire of *The Simpsons* is a given. Humor will work better for some members of your group, while a serious presentation of the facts will work for others. Spend some time with your group noting similarities and differences.)

Other Possible Activities
Environmental Impact Assessment

Obviously, you and your group will not be able to do any kind of comprehensive environmental impact survey as part of a lock-in or weekend retreat, but you can do a simplified assessment of the environmental impact of your church's building and grounds.

Divide the group into teams of no more than five or six persons. These teams will tour the church buildings and grounds and note anything that may have an environmental impact, either positive or negative. The teams can note simple things like what kind of light bulbs the church uses or how much plastic and foam products are used in the kitchen or fellowship hall. Does the church currently recycle? What kinds of chemicals and cleaning products does the church use? Is the church convenient for people to get there by bicycle? Can people get there by mass transit? What kind of appliances does the church use? Are they energy efficient? Is conservation of electricity and water encouraged? Your groups will likely see many other ways in which your church impacts the environment. If you want a more comprehensive list of what to look for, *Checklist for Green Congregations: Buildings, Grounds, and Practices* can be downloaded from the Web of Creation Web site at http://www.webofcreation .org/ActionSuggestions/Eco-Manual%20Checklist.doc. Or read the book *50 Ways to Help Save the Earth: An Action Guide for You and Your Church* by Rebecca Barnes-Davies. Your group may want to lead the congregation in becoming a "greener" community.

Tree Planting/Tree Garden

Plant a tree during the course of the retreat. It might be a way of memorializing someone or simply responding to the need for a tree in a certain area. Before doing this you will need to consult the grounds committee or other governing body of your church that approves such additions. If you have an appropriate size space you can plant a group of trees or a "tree garden." The trees can be grouped in a variety of ways. One way is to create a shade tree garden. In a shade tree garden the trees are planted in such a way that when they become fully mature they will provide a large area of shade where benches, chairs, or even a table can be placed so that the area can be used for outdoor relaxation, contemplation, meditation, and study. Another option is to plant a flowering tree garden, a group of trees chosen for their beauty when they bloom. A third option is to plant a small orchard of fruit trees (even three or four would be enough). For instance, if you lived in Florida you might plant a group of citrus trees with the understanding that when the trees fully mature the fruit will be harvested for a local food bank or program that feeds the homeless. Consult a local nursery to find trees indigenous to your area. You will also need expert advice about the special needs trees might have as you plant them and the appropriate spacing of the trees to accomplish your purpose.

Solitude in Nature

A green retreat is obviously well suited for an outdoor environment, and you could hold it at a local camp or go camping together as a group. However, you don't need to go camping to find a local park with a beautiful natural area or a nature path. The object of this activity is not just to "be in nature" but also to be in solitude while experiencing nature. Solitude is the spiritual discipline of being intentionally absent or isolated from other people and other things so that you can intensify your sense of the presence of God. Silence is also an important component of true solitude. In today's culture there are few opportunities to truly experience the spiritual power of silence. You will want to set aside about an hour and have scouted an area where each member of the group can spread out, find a place to be, and relax quietly. You can have a devotional contemplation guide prepared, or you can trust the members of your group to fill their own times of solitude. Encourage the members of the group to try to experience the natural setting with all five senses. What do they see? What do they hear? What do they smell? Once the time of solitude is finished, gather the group members so they can share testimonies about their experiences.

Mount Junk Mail

This activity requires some advance planning. For a week or so before the retreat, have members of the group save every piece of junk mail or paper advertisement they receive. You can also ask the church office to participate as well. Include the advertising sections of local newspapers and even car or door flyers if you wish. Have each member of the group bring his or her sack of junk mail to the retreat. At an appropriate moment ask members to take turns dumping the contents of their sacks at a central point in the meeting room and watch "Mount Junk Mail" rise from the floor. For an even more dramatic effect, members of the group might ask friends and neighbors to save their junk mail as well. The purpose of this activity is to illustrate how much paper we use (and often waste) on a daily basis.

Field Trip to a Recycling Plant

Plan an educational trip to a local recycling plant. Research your area to find a recycling plant that will agree to a tour, preferably with a guide. Types of recycling plants include paper, plastic, aluminum, other metals, asphalt, concrete, and glass.

Go Gleaning to Begin Greening

Gleaning is the gathering of crops left in the field after a mechanical harvest. When they have their first gleaning experience, people are often amazed at how much of a crop can be wasted. The Society of St. Andrew (http://www.endhunger.org) has led the way in this dynamic ministry. Its Web site can direct you to the closest office, organization, or persons in your area that coordinate gleaning ministry events.

Field Trip to Witness Pollution Firsthand

Research your area and find a site where pollution can be witnessed firsthand. This can be a lake, a river, an industrial site—any place where pollutants are introduced into the environment. You may even be able to find local organizations or environmental agencies that will give you a tour of various sites in your area and describe what is (or isn't) being done to make changes.

Clean Up and "Green Up"

Plan a "cleanup" trip to a local river, lake, park, abandoned lot, or other natural area. Often cleanup projects will be promoted in your community and you can be part of an even larger effort. This requires preparation to deal with disposal of the waste products and to provide safety for the participants. This is why it is often best to participate in a cleanup effort coordinated by a local agency, city, county, or municipality. Most cities have "Adopt a Road" programs to control litter along city streets. Your group or church may want to adopt a road to keep litter free.

Three-Legged Tree-Hugger Relay

Choose two trees close together and approximately the same distance from your starting line. Pair off the members of your group and have them prepare themselves for a traditional three-legged race. Group the pairs into two teams, and have the teams gather at the starting line. The goal is for each pair to run to its team's tree, hug it, and then return to the starting line to tag the next pair. The race is finished when every pair has hugged its team's tree and returned to the starting line (which is also the finish line). Try to downplay competition and emphasize cooperation and fun during the race.

Group Hug for a Tree

Find a tree in your area that is far too large for one person to hug (the larger the better). Have members of your group (or the whole group) join hands to encircle the tree and then move forward for a giant group "tree hug." You can use this as an opening activity for a "green" devotion or worship service. Most areas have a well-publicized, old-growth tree or stand of trees that is easily accessible.

Which Tree Hugged Me?

Find an area where there are several easily accessible trees with a relatively level open area between them. Divide the group into teams of two. One person is blindfolded and the other person becomes her guide. Have the guide lead her blindfolded partner to a particular tree. Encourage the blindfolded person to learn as much as he can about the tree by exploring the parts of the tree that he is able to reach. After a minute or two have the guide lead the blindfolded person back to where they began. Remove the blindfold and have the person who was wearing it try to locate the tree he "hugged" using only what he learned about the tree while blindfolded. Have the partners reverse roles.

This activity is a condensation of an environmental education activity created by James Neill. To see the details of his instructions for this activity and safety tips, go to http://wilderdom.com/games/descriptions/HugATree.html.

Prayer

Creator God, we worship you as the One who creates and re-creates his people. In a world that is slowly waking up to its duty of care for the creation, slowly becoming aware of the damage we inflict upon the planet, beginning to fear for the future of the earth, let the disturbing truth become ever more clear, in order that a deeper hope may become ever more real. In a world where talking about our environment fails to lead to action, where bold pledges are shallow publicity stunts, where urgent steps are postponed because of their political cost, let our lives reflect our claims in order that our promises ring true. In a world where guilt or indifference or despair prevent us from being stewards of the creation and worthy heralds of the gospel, let us worship our Creator in Spirit and in truth, in order that our lives and the life of the world may be remade. Lord God of heaven and earth, who was creating and is creating, make our lives into signs of hope that point to you, the Creator and Redeemer of the world. Amen. (An Environment

Day Prayer from http://www.baptist.org.uk/Resources/
resource_downloads/286.pdf)

Suggested Music
Melissa Etheridge, "I Need to Wake Up"

Melissa Etheridge won the Oscar for Best Original Song for this
theme from *An Inconvenient Truth*. Lyrics and guitar chords are
available online if you would like to use this song as a part of your
retreat.

Something to Talk About: Green Spirituality Web sites

The Web sites of the following organizations have a wealth of
resources for individuals and congregations wanting to become
more active in the movement toward "green spirituality." Most of
these sites suggest a wide variety of activities that could be used in
a lock-in or retreat setting.

> Web of Creation: Ecology Resources Transforming Faith
> and Society (http://webofcreation.org).
> Catholic Conservation Center (http://conservation.catholic
> .org). The mission of the center is to promote ecology,
> environmental justice, and the stewardship of creation.
> Earth Ministry (http://www.earthministry.org). Earth Min-
> istry's mission is to inspire and mobilize the Christian
> community to play a leadership role in building a just and
> sustainable future.
> Evangelical Environmental Network (http://www.creation
> care.org).
> Mennonite Creation Care Network (http://www.menno
> creationcare.org).
> Earth Care Online (http://www.earthcareonline.org) is a
> Christian organization that exists to promote creation
> stewardship within the Christian community.
> The National Religious Partnership for the Environment
> (http://www.nrpe.org) is an association of independent
> faith groups across a broad spectrum.

The Association for Environmental and Outdoor Education
has a list of resources for spiritual environmental education (http://aeoe.org/resources/spiritual/index.html).

10 "Revenge of Nature" Movies that will add a Little Fun to Your Green Retreat (and even contribute to the discussion if you wish)

- *The Day after Tomorrow* (2004, 124 minutes, PG-13). This is Roland Emmerich's look at what might happen if all of our worst fears about global warming were realized, well, the day after tomorrow.

- *The Happening* (2008, 91 minutes, R, original working title "The Green Effect"). Written and directed by M. Night Shyamalan, this is a bizarre look at what might happen if the earth itself went vigilante in order to rid itself of the human threat. Caution: this film is rated R for intensely violent and disturbing images. It is gruesome at points and is probably only suited for older youth and adults.

- *Frogs* (1972, 91 minutes, PG). This is a wonderful, old, campy movie that's high on the "eeewww" factor. On an island owned by an eccentric millionaire, amphibians, reptiles, and insects band together to take vengeance on the humans trying to poison them out of existence.

- *The Birds* (1963, 119 minutes, PG-13). Why are all these birds pecking on us? Alfred Hitchcock presents this classic metaphor for the unexplained and pervasive presence of evil in the world.

- *The China Syndrome* (1979, 122 minutes, PG). Jack Lemmon and Jane Fonda were nominated for Oscars in this fast-paced cautionary tale about the safety of nuclear reactors.

- *Silkwood* (1984, 131 minutes, R). Meryl Streep and Cher were both nominated as Best Actress for their roles in this Mike Nichols film about safety at a plutonium processing plant.

Streep plays Karen Silkwood, a metallurgy worker at the plant who was (allegedly) purposefully contaminated by radiation, psychologically tortured, and quite possibly murdered to prevent her from exposing blatant worker safety violations at the plant.

- *Erin Brockovich* (2000, 130 minutes, R). Julia Roberts took home the Best Actress Oscar for her cinematic portrayal of real-life eco-heroine Erin Brockovich. In the film, Brockovich, a single mom, takes a job as a legal assistant and winds up bringing down a major power company that has been contaminating the local watershed with deadly toxic waste.

- *Soylent Green* (1973, 97 minutes, PG). Overpopulation is the ecological threat in this campy sci-fi thriller starring Charlton Heston. In the future, the earth is severely overpopulated, and Heston, playing a New York police detective, finds himself marked for murder by government agents when he gets too close to a horrible state secret involving the origins of a revolutionary, badly needed, and tasty new food source. The film has one of the great "one-liner" endings in the history of the movies.

- *A Civil Action* (1998, 115 minutes, PG-13). In another film loosely based on the life of an actual eco-hero, John Travolta plays Jan Schlichtmann, a successful attorney who agrees to represent eight families from Woburn, Massachusetts, whose children died from leukemia after two large corporations leaked toxic chemicals into the water supply. He continues to pursue the case even when it brings him to the edge of financial ruin and career suicide.

- *Fire Down Below* (1997, 105 minutes, R). OK, yes, it is a Steven Segal movie. Segal plays EPA agent Jack Taggart, who is fighting a big business that has been dumping toxic waste into abandoned mineshafts in Kentucky. Although the film gets a bit preachy, it has enough martial arts and action to be fun and enough environmental emphasis to be useful.

Two Great "Greenies" for the Younger Crowd

- *Free Willy* **(1993, 112 minutes, PG).** In this classic, feel-good tale, a twelve-year-old boy learns that a beloved killer whale is about to be euthanized by aquarium owners. To free the whale, the boy risks everything.

- *Hoot* **(2006, 91 minutes, PG).** In this film, based on a youth novel by South Florida writer and environmental crusader Carl Hiaasen, a young man moves from Montana to Florida with his family, where he teams up with a tough girl in a fight to protect a population of endangered owls.

More Green Documentaries Anyone?
(That is, if An Inconvenient Truth *wasn't enough for you)*

- *Who Killed the Electric Car?* **(2006, 92 minutes, PG).** In 1996, fully electric cars produced primarily by GM began to appear on roads all over California. They were quiet and fast, produced no exhaust, and ran without gasoline, yet ten years later these cars were gathered up and crushed. This is the fascinating story of a corporate mystery that flies in the face of environmental common sense. The straightforward, simple presentation of this film makes it a great choice to use with younger youth.

- *Blue Vinyl* **(2002, 98 minutes, unrated).** When acclaimed documentary filmmaker Judith Hefland tries to convince her parents to get rid of the blue vinyl siding on their house, she begins a quest with fellow filmmaker Daniel B. Gold to the U.S. vinyl capital in Louisiana and beyond. Along the way they talk to doctors, scientists, experts, and activists about the dangers of the bioaccumulation of plastics in our environment.

- *The End of Suburbia: Oil Depletion and the Collapse of the American Dream* **(2004, 78 minutes, unrated).** If you didn't

fall asleep reading the title, you'll find this prophetic documentary quite compelling. The film explores the end of cheap oil,
suburbia, and the resource-intensive "American Dream," accu-
rately predicting the economic crisis in which we now find
ourselves.

Five

Sacrament and Sacrilege: An Appreciation of *The Simpsons Movie*

Mark I. Pinsky

Several weeks before *The Simpsons Movie* was released in July 2007, Matt Groening and several other creative lights from the show hosted a London screening of a ten-minute segment of the film. Afterward, a reporter asked screenwriter and longtime executive producer Al Jean about the clip's suggestion of religious content, especially in light of the fact that Rowan Williams, archbishop of Canterbury, is an outspoken fan of the show. Jean replied that he hoped that the church would not be offended. "We posit the existence of an extremely active God," he said, adding cryptically, "I don't think the archbishop will be disappointed."[1]

While God makes no physical appearance in *The Simpsons Movie*, as he does in several television episodes, Williams probably wasn't disappointed, nor were the millions of others who saw the film. By its second weekend, the movie—whose promotional ads promised "irreverent humor throughout"—had generated a U.S. box office of more than $128 million and a worldwide total of $315 million. Many of the religious and spiritual elements present in the show's previous eighteen seasons are present in the movie, if only in shorthand. But they are there mainly for those who are alert to them—and not to those who aren't. For those who have the eyes—and the inclination—to see faith in *The Simpsons Movie*, it is there.

In an early scene, for example, Homer tries to do good by rescuing a cute animal from needless slaughter, but his thoughtlessness and disregard of the common good of the town lead to disaster. In the process, he also ignores his family's needs, especially those of his son, Bart. The reality of human frailty and the promise of redemption and reconciliation, as hard as they may be at times, are the overarching themes that play out through the rest of the film.

Faith versus Organized Religion

As in the TV show, sincere faith is handled with a light and sympathetic touch. Other themes that run through the movie, as in the series, are that genuine belief should be respected, while organized religion is suspect and subject to ridicule. Many of the familiar elements from the show—Homer's confusion and disappointment with religion; the fickleness and inconstancy of personal devotion; the essential goodness of Ned Flanders, the evangelical next-door neighbor; and even wacky church signs—are all on display in the movie.

Organized religion does get the back of the movie's hand. As disaster looms, church worshipers flee the sanctuary and run to Moe's bar next door; patrons of the tavern, fearing the end is near, stampede to the church, where the smug sign outside later reads, "We Told You So." Early in the film, in just a few scenes and lines of dialogue, Homer demonstrates his contempt for the church, as well as his extremely hazy understanding of Christian theology and his disdain for formal worship. Arriving late to a memorial service at the First Church of Springfield for the rock group Green Day, Homer tells his family their entrance is unlikely to be noticed, since "those pious morons are too busy praying to their phony baloney God." He explains that he wishes he could pray his own way and rely on his practical plan B for personal salvation, a version of Pascal's wager: "Praying like hell when I'm on my deathbed." Overheard by the congregation, he tries to recover, offering the peace of the Lord to all, only to confuse Jesus with "Jebus," a familiar error obsessive fans of the show will recall.

Speaking of obsessive, some particularly acute observers, such as Canadian pop culture expert David Buckna, spotted what they think are more obscure religious references. When Homer illegally dumps a silo of pig manure into Lake Springfield, the license plate on the back of his car reads, "1PHL07." "As soon as I saw the plate, I figured it had to be either 1 Philippians, verse 7, or 1 Philemon, verse 7," Buckna said. "When you read the KJV of Philemon, verse 7, one can surmise that the Simpsons writers are having a little fun with the 'KJV only' crowd. In the King James Version, Philemon 1:7 reads: 'For we have great joy and consolation in thy love, because the bowels of the saints are refreshed by thee, brother.'" Buckna then added, "That said, 'bowel' does not refer to 'intestine,' but to 'heart'—typically defined as the center of one's being and emotions."[2]

A modern translation, such as the New International Version, reads, "Your love has given me great joy and encouragement, because you, brother, have refreshed the hearts of the saints."

Christian Reviews and Reaction

In its review, the evangelical magazine *Christianity Today* gave the film a mixed evaluation. "Christianity is mocked a few times in the movie, but it's not a mean-spirited agenda, more an indictment of religion than faith," according to Russ Breimeier, a fan of the television show. The movie "takes shots at everyone and everything, including the Christian church," he wrote, "which is mostly why I don't get too worked up when the humor wanders into sacrilege. Though nothing is sacred, nothing escapes their crosshairs either. . . . And despite poking fun at the exaggerated straightlaced qualities of Ned Flanders, this film truly loves the Simpson neighbor for honorably showing love to others in need. . . . Like Harry Potter and many other cultural sensations the Simpsons have long been cause for division among Christians." Yet, in the end, what the movie "is poking fun at is how Christians behave sometimes, like when we are overly pious, or our responses to things in culture," Breimeier told Christopher Quinn of the *Atlanta Journal-Constitution*.[3]

Some of the film's antics "will prove too much for some Christian fans of the show, while others may see them, in context, as meaningful satire," wrote Christian Hamaker, of crosswalk.com. "Both camps will find plenty to laugh at—or plenty to be offended by—depending on their tolerance for *The Simpsons'* stock blend of sarcasm, satire and skewering of political correctness. That's the same tightwire the show has always walked. Many Christians have had a love/hate relationship with the pop-culture phenomenon since it debuted in the late 1980s."[4] A reviewer for the Catholic News Service called the movie "uplifting." "Director David Silverman generates plenty of chuckles, but for all the foolery and family dysfunction, there's an underlying pro-family agenda, and the satiric jibes are generally not malicious."[5]

Of course, there were some Christians who didn't need to see how they were treated on the big screen to express their disdain for *The Simpsons Movie.* In a survey conducted by ChristiaNet, 51 percent of those polled said they felt the movie was not appropriate for Christians. A majority of the 570 Christians responding to the survey had not seen the movie but based their opinion on the TV show, according to Bill Cooper, president of ChristiaNet. "It is refreshing to see that the majority of Christians can discern when entertainment is crossing the line," he said in a press release, sounding a lot like Ned Flanders. Seventeen percent of those polled said they felt *The Simpsons* was appropriate for Christian viewers, while 32 percent said they were unsure. Many said they had never watched a single episode of the show.[6]

This is particularly unfortunate, because faith gets a sympathetic and understanding ride on the television series, as it has for the past two decades. One of the chief gifts of the long-running, award-winning series is that the characters' fundamental beliefs are animated but not caricatured. Heartfelt faith is not questioned. God is not mocked, nor is God's existence questioned. (When God appears, usually in a dream, as in the Bible, he doesn't have four fingers, as have other cartoon characters since the emergence of Disney, but five. And his countenance is never revealed.) More than any other show on commercial television, *The Simpsons* mirrors the faith lives and practices of most Americans. In the television series at least, the family says grace at meals, goes to church on Sundays, and reads and refers to the Bible. They pray aloud and believe God answers their prayers. Ned Flanders has become the best-known (and loved) evangelical in the country, at least among young people. Still, no one would mistake Homer Simpson and his family for saints. In many ways, in fact, they are quintessentially weak, well-meaning sinners who rely on their faith—although only when absolutely necessary. True to its reputation, and as the Christian reviewers note, *The Simpsons* is consistently irreverent toward organized religion's failings and excesses, as it is with most other institutions and aspects of modern life.

Scores of churches have made or intend to make extensive use of *The Simpsons*, both in North America and in England. Hundreds of churches and college classes have used the first edition of this guide, and the Church of England announced in 2007 it intends to publish its own study guide, *Mixing It Up with the Simpsons*. The guide will be distributed to all Anglican Church youth leaders in Britain, according to the *Christian Post*, in order "to provide a more relevant way of teaching children about theology and to give a boost to dwindling congregations."[7] Relevant episodes of the show will be screened as part of the course.

The Spirit Moving?

A strong suggestion of divine inspiration propels *The Simpsons Movie*'s plot and suggests its resolution. At the memorial service, which is packed, the normally unctuous Reverend Lovejoy prays, "Let the Lord's light shine upon you." The minister asks the congregation to "feel the spirit" and calls on the Lord to "hear our prayers." In fact, they are heard—and answered—in an atypical turn toward the supernatural and the ecstatic for the normally staid, mainline Protestant church. A beam of heavenly sunlight, shining through one of the sanctuary's stained-glass windows, transports Grampa Simpson into a prophetic trance (albeit one with Three Stooges overtones). His extended bout of glossolalia, speaking in tongues, sends him thrashing around on the floor as if he were a charismatic, "slain in the Spirit."

In light of the seizure, Homer's first impulse is to flip through his Bible for guidance, only to conclude, "This book doesn't have any answers." Some reviewers see considerable significance in this Pentecostal moment. "The early scene in which Grandpa Simpson collapses in church and begins uttering prophecies seems to me like nothing I'd ever seen on the TV show," writes Peter Sanderson in a feature called "Comics in Context," on the Web site Quick Stop Entertainment. "Yes, on the surface the scene was played for laughs, and yet the prophecies came true. It was as if by ignoring Grandpa's warnings (which he didn't understand anyway), Homer was defying fate, thereby causing the disaster that befell Springfield. Perhaps *The Simpsons Movie* writers were intentionally parodying 'end of the world' movies, and therefore were parodying the trope of the Cassandra-like warnings that go ignored. Still, the prophecies prepare us for the supernatural doings later in the movie."[8]

But Marge, always the family's true believer—in the movie asking God in needlepoint to bless her home—tries her best to interpret Grampa's ravings. She is disappointed on the ride home from church when other family members do not share her faith. "What is the point of going to church every Sunday if someone we love has a genuine religious experience and we just ignore it?" she asks. Later she reminds them, "What happened in church was a warning. . . . Something happened to that man."

Ned Flanders has a prominent role in *The Simpsons Movie*, as he does in the series. In a prerelease interview with National Public Radio, Groening acknowledged the temptation to take cheap shots at a Christian character like Flanders but said, "It would be too easy,"[9] so the writers chose not to. In the movie, he is portrayed with a sympathetic three-dimensionality, which raises the emotional stakes for the viewer—a part of what has made *The Simpsons* so addictive for so many years. That comes through in the movie version, Mark Moring, of christianitytoday.com, told the *Atlanta Journal-Constitution*. "Ned Flanders is actually portrayed more closely to one of us than [in] a lot of other movies," especially those that stereotype evangelicals as self-righteous party-poopers, he said. "He is actually a nice guy, which is what evangelicals want to be known for."[10]

In the movie, Flanders is presented as a devoted single father who says grace with his children at a fast-food restaurant and even carries a spare pair of boys' pants (which he offers to an indisposed Bart) because he knows their knees wear out from praying. Although literal-minded and narrow, he risks his own life to save the Simpson family from an angry lynch mob, explaining, "We're neighbors." An exemplary Christian, he also serves as a caring father figure for Bart when Homer ignores his son, but he urges the boy to return to his real father when Homer tries to make amends.

Flanders's overzealous beliefs are not immune from satire, however, his exemplary personal life notwithstanding. When he sees a pollution-mutated squirrel with a thousand eyes, he marvels, "Who am I to question the work of the Almighty?" It is, he concludes, a manifestation of "mighty fine Intelligent Design." Flanders's faith is unshaken as Springfield faces annihilation. He takes his children to the church, where they are alone in the sanctuary, and prepares them for the end. "When you meet Jesus, be sure to call him 'Mr. Christ,'" he tells them.

"Will Buddha be there?" one of the boys asks. "No!" he snaps, with characteristic intolerance of any non-Judeo-Christian faith. As the end nears, he and his boys pray confidently on their doorstep. There are several other nods toward religious diversity in the movie, as when Homer is guided by an Eskimo shaman and a cluster of speaking trees, reminiscent of characters in animated Disney features like *Brother Bear* and *Pocahontas*. After a session of throat singing, the shaman tells Homer he will be redeemed only when he has an "epiphany" (which she has to define, naturally).

For Homer, that revelation is simple: "Other people are just as important as me." When divine inspiration is again called for, it comes at the direction of a branch of one of these ethereal trees. As residents of Springfield celebrate their deliverance, Apu is about to kiss his wife when the scene is blocked by Homer's motorcycle—in apparent deference to Hindu tradition and Bollywood movie convention.

In the end, Homer and Marge ride off together, bathed in reconciliation's divine light. By no stretch of interpretation was *The Simpsons Movie* a film about religion. Like the TV show, it was about a family and a community in which religion plays a part. Nothing more, nothing less. In a recent print "interview" with *USA Today*, Homer explains his theology this way: "Every time I see my sweet girl Lisa, I believe in God. Every time I see Bart, I believe in the devil."[11]

Notes

1. Adam Sherwin, "Bart Shows Fans the Unexpected as Simpson Film Beats Censor with a Yellow Streak," *Times* (London), July 6, 2007, 32.
2. E-mail interview with author, August 2, 2007.
3. Russ Breimeier, quoted by Christopher Quinn, "Author Ponders 'What Would Flanders Do?'" *Atlanta Journal-Constitution*, August 3, 2007, 1E.
4. Christian Hamaker, "Fans, Foes Will Find Plenty of Ammo in 'The Simpsons Movie,'" http://www.crosswalk.com/movies/11549246.
5. Catholic News Service, http://www.catholicherald.com/articles/07articles/caps0712.html.
6. "The Simpsons Offend Christians according to ChristiaNet.com Poll," August 1, 2007, http://www.christiannewswire.com/news/272623785.html.
7. Eric Young, "Church of England Recruits Simpsons to Teach Theology, Boost Attendance," *Palm Beach Post*, August 4, 2007, 1A.
8. Peter Sanderson, Comics in Context, http://www.quickstopentertainment.com/2007/08/03/comics-in-context-188-dohme.
9. Matt Groening, *Morning Edition*, National Public Radio, July 26, 2007.
10. Mark Moring, quoted in Quinn, "Author Ponders 'What Would Flanders Do?'" 1E.
11. Scott Bowles, "A Sit-Down with Simpson," *USA Today*, July 26, 2007, 2D.

Futurama

Six

The Nature of God

Futurama Episode: "Godfellas"

Synopsis: When Bender tries to nap in an empty torpedo tube during a battle with space pirates, he is inadvertently shot out into space. Unable to catch up with him or find him, Leela and Fry reluctantly head home. Fry spends hours searching the heavens for any sign of his friend, but to no avail, as the telescopes he's using just aren't strong enough. Fry then learns that a group of monks is using the world's most powerful radio telescope to search for God. He and Leela head to the monastery in hopes of getting a chance to use the telescope. As Bender hurtles through space he flies into an asteroid field and is bombarded by the space rocks. Two of the rocks that strike him contain tiny civilizations. The civilization on his front side can see Bender's face and immediately declares him God. He tries to be a benevolent deity, but everything he attempts to do backfires, causing pain and suffering for his people. Eventually the "believers" on Bender's front side go to war with the "nonbelievers" on his backside and wipe each other out with nuclear weapons. Later it seems as if Bender actually encounters God in the form of a talking nebula. They have a conversation about how difficult it is to be God and get things right. Back on Earth, Fry and Leela lock the monks in a closet and seize the telescope. Just as they are leaving, the telescope scans over the nebula where Bender is, and the nebula, hearing Fry's call, transports Bender back to Earth.

Supplementary Reading: *The Gospel according to* The Simpsons, 2nd ed.: Afterword, *Futurama*, pp. 229–35

Old Testament Lesson: Ps. 8:3–5; Isa. 55:8–9

New Testament Lesson: Col. 1:15–22

Activity: Write the following phrase on a whiteboard or flip chart: "If I were God I would . . ." Make sure that all participants have something on which to write and a writing implement, and direct them to spend about five minutes completing this sentence by listing five things they would do if they could be God for a day. After they have finished, encourage members of the group to share what they have written. Direct the group in sorting through the types of responses they made. Some might be personal: "I would heal my mother's Alzheimer's disease." Some might be self-centered: "I'd make sure I won the lottery." Others might be altruistic: "I'd bring an end to genocide in Darfur." Some might even be vengeful or vindictive: "I'd make sure that so and so was punished for what he or she did." Ask the group: Would you make it clear that what you did as "God" was "divine intervention"? Do you think it would strengthen your faith more to know for certain that God had directly intervened to change something in the order of creation? Or is it more important that we discern God's actions in creation through our faith without direct knowledge that God has intervened? You can weave what is discovered here into your later discussions.

Questions for Discussion: Prior to the discussion, have a member of the group read aloud each of the Scripture lessons.

- How would you describe Bender's first encounter with the Shrimpkins? (Once the asteroids have attached themselves to Bender's body, the Shrimpkins immediately acknowledge him as their savior—"he who hath taken us unto his breast." Then they proceed to worship him as they all "bow before the Metal Lord." What's important about this is that Bender did not choose to be the Shrimpkins' god; the Shrimpkins gave him that idea when they started worshiping him. Of course, Bender,

The Baylor Religion Survey

The Baylor Institute for Studies of Religion and the Department of Sociology conducted the Baylor Religion Survey during the winter of 2005–2006. They asked 1,721 randomly selected American adults a total of 77 questions covering a broad range of religious questions. One question dealt with the existence of God in some detail. Participants were asked, "Which one statement comes closest to your personal beliefs about God?" The statements and the percentage of participants who chose that statement follow:

65.8 percent said, "I have no doubts that God exists."

14.3 percent said, "I believe in a higher power or cosmic force."

10.8 percent said, "I believe in God, but with some doubts."

4.6 percent said, "I don't believe in anything beyond the physical world."

2.8 percent said, "I have no opinion."

1.7 percent said, "I sometimes believe in God."

Another intriguing finding of the Baylor Study was a significant difference between how men and women view the importance of God in their lives. When asked to affirm or deny the following statement, "God is very important in my life," 63 percent of the participants affirmed that God was very important in their lives. However, when the results were broken down between men and women, a significant difference emerged: 75 percent of women affirmed that God was very important in their lives, as opposed to only 50 percent of the men.

The Four Ways People Perceive God

Another significant finding of the Baylor Religion Survey that has excited researchers is that people perceive God in four distinct ways depending on how engaged they think God is in the world and how angry God is with the world. The Baylor research team found that Americans are divided between four different perceptions of God, which they identified as "authoritarian," "benevolent," "critical," and "distant."

The data showed:

> 31.4 percent believe in an authoritarian God, who is very judgmental and engaged
>
> 25 percent believe in a benevolent God, who is not judgmental but engaged
>
> 23 percent believe in a distant God, who is completely removed
>
> 16 percent believe in a critical God, who is judgmental but not engaged

Professor Paul Froese of Baylor University observed, "This is a very powerful tool to understand core differences in the United States. If I know your image of God, I can tell all kinds of things about you. It's a central part of world view and it's linked to how you think about the world in general." Baylor's Christopher Bader goes even further: "You learn more about people's moral and political behavior if you know their image of God than almost any other measure. It turns out to be a more powerful predictor of social and political views than the usual markers of church attendance or belief in the Bible."

who could have denied the title, takes full advantage of the situation.)

- What are Bender's initial reactions to the Shrimpkins? (Bender first sees them as a distraction to break up the boredom of eternally drifting through space. Once he chooses a "prophet" [Malachi], he is able to communicate with them. Of course, Bender's self-centered worldview is revealed when the first action he takes is to shake Malachi down for his wallet. Bender is disappointed to find the people who worship him "are but a poor and simple folk." He then proceeds to "lay down a few commandments." In the end, Bender only has one commandment: "God needs booze.")

- Does the Shrimpkins' decision to devote their entire existence to producing beer for Bender remind you of the sacrifices and offerings Israel made to God before the final destruction of the second temple in Jerusalem by the Romans in 70 BCE? (In Hebrew, the word for "sacrifice" was *korban* [from the Hebrew root *karov*, which, loosely translated, means, "to come close to God"]. The ancient Hebrews saw sacrifices as a way to atone for their sins and appease God. As a primarily agricultural people [like the Shrimpkins], the Hebrews sacrificed animals from their herds and flocks, but they also made offerings to God of other agricultural commodities such as grains, oils, fruits, bread, incense, and wine. Microbrew would not be that much different from wine. At the time of Jesus, the sacrificial system was still the center of Jewish religious life.)

- What are the results of Bender's commandment? (The entire purpose of existence for the Shrimpkin civilization now centers around making beer for Bender. When Bender discovers that Malachi has lost an arm, Malachi informs him that most of the Shrimpkins were injured or maimed in the building of the "great brewery." Further, many Shrimpkins died from the toxic air pollution produced by the plant. On top of that, Malachi informs Bender, "the liquor industry attracted organized crime.")

- How does Bender respond to the suffering of the Shrimpkins? He tells Malachi to inform the people that "the Lord is moved by their plight." However, when Bender begins to cry, a single tear falls on the Shrimpkin world and hits it like a tsunami, wiping out everything in its path and sweeping away Malachi's son, Malachi Jr. Bender sees this and reaches down to rescue the boy.)

- How do the Shrimpkins respond to Bender's miraculous act in saving Malachi Jr.? (Once they see Bender work a miracle on Malachi's behalf, they all want miracles of their own. Bender's miracles don't work out so well for the Shrimpkins. One village prays for wealth and is crushed when Bender flips a coin on them. Another village asks for sunshine to help their barley grow, but Bender ends up burning all of their fields and setting several of the farmers on fire.)

- What is Bender's next strategy for dealing with the Shrimpkins? (He gives them a "bible" and decides not to interfere with the Shrimpkins at all. Left to their own devices, the Shrimpkins decide to "convert the unbelievers" on Bender's backside. Both of the civilizations tap into Bender's nuclear pile and vaporize each other with atomic weapons.)

- Do you think that the talking nebula Bender encounters is God? (It seems the writers of this episode wanted to lead us to that conclusion. In fact, in screenplay transcriptions the nebula's character is identified as "God." The talking nebula is actually an allusion to the beginning of the famous Frank Capra movie *It's a Wonderful Life*. At the beginning of that movie God speaks to George Bailey's guardian angel from a nebula.)

- What does Bender learn in his conversation with the nebula? (The two discuss God's nature, how difficult it is to deal with prayers ["so many asking for so much"], and the best way to relate to a people if you are "God." The nebula tells Bender, "Being God isn't easy. If you do too much, people get dependent. And if you do nothing, they lose hope. You have to use a light touch." At the conclusion of the episode, Bender chooses to do the right thing and save the monks himself because, he observes, "you can't count on God for jack. He pretty much told me so himself." However, as Bender leaves to rescue the monks the nebula says, "When you do things right, people won't be sure you've done anything at all.")

- Have the class look at the four ways that people perceive God according to the researchers in the Baylor Religion Study. Which of these four perceptions best describes Bender's relationship with the Shrimpkins? Which of these four perceptions best describes the nebula in relationship to Bender? Do you think that the writers of this episode wanted us to come to a conclusion about the nature of God? (All this depends on personal interpretation; however, we can make some general observations. It can be argued that at different stages of his relationship with the Shrimpkins Bender exhibits attributes of all four ways of seeing God: authoritarian, benevolent, critical, and distant. The concluding theological statement of the nebula puts God solidly in the category of a benevolent God, who is not judgmental but engaged. However, the nebula intimates that at times God may have exhibited the other three qualities as well.)

- What do Psalm 8:3–5 and Isaiah 55:8–9 have to say about our relationship to and perception of God? (The Psalms passage states the awesome sovereignty of God in relation to human beings. Yet the psalmist does not see God as "distant," "removed," or "not engaged." Instead, the psalmist celebrates the overwhelming reality that despite the ultimate transcendence of God, human beings can experience God in intimate and deeply personal ways. At first, some may feel that Isaiah is emphasizing the "distance" between God and human beings. However, this verse doesn't deny God's engagement with human beings; it simply states that there are aspects of God's nature that human beings will never truly be able to understand because of our finite nature.)

- What do you think the writer of Colossians 1:15–22 wants us to conclude about God? (This is one of the key passages for understanding Paul's perception of God in all his letters. First, Paul makes it a point to connect God and Jesus infinitely and eternally. The passage begins with a litany of God's sovereign attributes but moves quickly from the ultimate transcendence of God to God's complete personal engagement with creation through Jesus of Nazareth. There can be no more complete an engagement than the "fullness of God . . . pleased to dwell in human form." Paul tells us that while God is infinitely transcendent, God is also radically immanent in a profoundly personal way. Ultimately, Paul says, God's goal is to redeem all of God's creation through God's unconditional love and grace, "to reconcile to himself all things, whether on earth or in heaven, by making peace through the blood of his cross." It would be difficult to posit a deeper level of engagement with human beings than this.)

Prayer: God our Creator, thank you for being mindful of us and caring for us. Guide us in understanding you better so that we might experience your love more deeply. We admit that we sometimes have questions and doubts. Remind us that your thoughts are not always our thoughts and that your ways are not always our ways. Yet, despite that, we know that you will continue to be as completely present to us as is possible for our experience. Help us to love others as you have loved us, that we might be instruments of your desire to redeem all of your creation. Amen.

Something to Talk About: There are two movies in particular that cover much of the same ground as this episode of *Futurama* and would be great to use if you wanted to expand this session into a weekend retreat format.

- *Bruce Almighty* (2003, 101 minutes, PG-13). Bruce Nolan (Jim Carrey) is a television reporter in Buffalo, New York, who seems to get the worst possible stories and fears he will be passed over for a promotion. Despite his local celebrity status and the love of his girlfriend, Grace (Jennifer Aniston), Bruce is unhappy with almost every aspect of his life. At the end of a really bad day, Bruce blames his problems on God's inability to do his job right. God shows up in human form (Morgan Freeman) and endows Bruce with all his divine powers for a week, challenging him to do the job better if he can. Turmoil ensues as Bruce's ineptitude in using his new powers wreaks havoc in the world around him. While trying to get everything he ever wanted, he ends up losing the thing he loves the most.

- *Oh, God!* **(1977, 98 minutes, PG).** God reveals himself as an unassuming old man (George Burns) to Jerry Landers (John Denver), the assistant manager of a grocery store. God informs Jerry that, like Moses, he has been chosen to be God's messenger to the contemporary world. Not that comfortable with his newfound status as God's "prophet," Jerry dutifully tells the world the story of his encounters with God. As Jerry tries to get the message across, everyone around him begins to believe he's crazy. Even his dedicated and loving wife Bobbie (Teri Garr) begins to doubt his sanity. Charging that Jerry is a fraud, a group of theologians challenges Jerry to prove that God exists in court. The end is reminiscent of a favorite Christmas movie—*Miracle on 34th Street.*

Seven

What about Hell?

Futurama Episode: "Hell Is Other Robots"

Synopsis: When Bender begins experimenting with receiving massive jolts of electricity to alter his mind, he eventually finds himself hopelessly addicted. In desperation, he joins the Church of Robotology and converts to their strict code of moral and ethical conduct. When Bender then becomes overbearingly self-righteous and sanctimonious, his friends tempt him back to his old "sinful" ways. After a night of debauchery in Atlantic City, Bender finds himself in robot hell. Feeling guilty, Fry and Leela go searching for Bender and find that robot hell actually exists in an abandoned amusement park. They end up literally "storming the gates of hell" to rescue their friend.

Supplementary Reading: *The Gospel according to* The Simpsons, 2nd ed.: Afterword, *Futurama*, pp. 229–35

Old Testament Lesson: Ps. 139:7–12

New Testament Lesson: Luke 16:19–31

Epistle Lesson: Rom. 5:20–6:2

Activity: Write the following on a whiteboard or flip chart: "Hell for me would be . . ." Make sure that all participants have something on which to write and a writing implement, and direct them to spend about five minutes completing this sentence. Emphasize that they should be creative and not stick to traditional ideas about hell. This exercise is designed to get them to "personalize" the idea of hell from their own individual points of view. After they have finished writing, encourage members of the group to share what they have written. Stress the need for open-mindedness and that no one should be teased or ridiculed about what he or she has written. Use what is shared here as a transition to discussing the conventional perceptions of hell that will be discussed later.

Questions for Discussion: Prior to the discussion, have a member of the group read aloud each of the Scripture lessons.

- What does Bender do to get himself sent to robot hell? (Bender is a heavy drinker, smoker, womanizer, and gambler. He also is a chronic kleptomaniac. However, none of this is the reason he winds up in hell. Bender starts abusing electricity to alter his consciousness. It turns out to be the robot equivalent of heroin. He is soon hopelessly addicted and spends his time searching for his next fix of high-voltage juice. To break free from his addiction he joins the Church of Robotology and commits to their rigid standards of moral and ethical behavior. When he violates his baptismal vow, he finds himself in hell.)

- What are the signs of Bender's addiction, and why don't his friends realize that he is in trouble? (Bender is a wild man . . . er . . . bot. He does just about everything he enjoys to excess. In fact, his name is a play on words. He is called Bender because he is designed to bend steel girders, but people often call a drinking binge a "bender." Of course, Bender claims his alcohol abuse is necessary to fuel him and keep him running efficiently. To this point his excessive behaviors haven't caused him too many problems. Once he starts abusing electricity, however, he exhibits the classic behaviors associated with addiction: He lives in a fantasy world and lies about his behavior to himself and others. He feels that he "needs" the electricity to relieve stress and make him happy. He has a false sense that the electricity is actually helping him take control of the negative aspects of his life, but ultimately, his addiction becomes self-destructive. As with many people who have friends with an addiction, Bender's friends are in denial. They see the symptoms but fail to do anything to stop Bender.)

- What are some of the forms that Bender's self-destructive impulses take? (He puts himself and others in harm's way in order to get more "juice." He steals electricity at work. He betrays his friends. He is in despair and feels he is a worthless

---

No Exit: "Hell Is Other People"

The title for this *Futurama* episode, "Hell Is Other Robots," is a play on one of Jean Paul Sartre's most famous dramatic lines. "Hell is other people" (in French, "*l'enfer, c'est les autres*") is found in what is perhaps Sartre's most famous play, *No Exit.*

No Exit begins with a valet leading a character named Garcin into a room that could be in any large apartment building or hotel. However, the audience soon realizes that Garcin is in hell. The room has only one door, no windows, and not even a mirror. After a short while two women, Inès and Estelle, join Garcin in the bleak little room. After Inès and Estelle arrive, the door is shut and locked behind them. The three expect that they will eventually be tortured, but no torturer ever appears. Gradually they begin to understand that they have been thrown together to torment each other. Their pain grows more intense as each probes the others' weaknesses, failings, sins, and desires. For a while they can visualize what is happening to those on earth, but their connection to those left behind begins to fade as the living go on with their lives. Eventually the three are left with only the intimacy of whatever they are thinking, their only companionship the other two. As the play draws to a close, Garcin demands to be released, and as he speaks the door bursts open. At first, it seems that they are free, but so much heat is coming through the open door that they choose the despair of remaining in the room together rather than breaking free. Even though the door is open, for them, hell has no exit because they refuse to leave.

"lost cause." He isolates himself until all he has is his addiction, and he even exhibits suicidal thoughts and tendencies.)

- How does Bender escape his addiction? (Bender converts to the Church of Robotology and is baptized in a barrel of high-viscosity oil. He vows to change his ways and walk the straight and narrow. As a symbol of Bender's vow, a resistor symbol is welded to his body.)

- What is Bender's life like after his conversion experience? (He becomes insufferably sanctimonious and self-righteous. He is moralistic, he insists on saying grace before meals and prays endless prayers in binary code, he attempts to coerce others into his lifestyle, and he demands "appropriate behaviors" from his friends. At one point, he even insists on a "group hug.")

- How do his friends react? (At first Bender's friends are supportive, but eventually they become frustrated and grow weary of the "new and improved" Bender. They want their old friend back. As a last-ditch effort they even try to sabotage Bender by taking him on a trip to Atlantic City, where they entice him with all his old excessive pursuits. It works; Bender backslides and winds up in robot hell.)

- What do you think Paul means in Romans 5:20–6:2 when he asks, "Should we continue in sin in order that grace may abound?" How does this apply to Bender? (Paul is saying that all human beings fall prey to their weakness and sin. The law does nothing to break this cycle, while grace, on the other hand, does. So in Paul's mind, the more human beings sin, the more grace becomes available to change their lives. Bender is not really living in grace; he is living his life in a moralistic way based on "rules." He needs to find grace and forgiveness in order to truly change spiritually.)

- What is robot hell like? (It has all the stereotypical features often associated with hell. It is run by the robot devil. It has fire and brimstone. It has levels of punishment as in Dante's *Inferno*. Worst of all, it's like being stuck in a bad musical forever!

The Three New Testament Words That Give Us Hell

Three words from the Gospels are translated to English as the word "hell."

Sheol
Sheol (pronounced "sheh-ole") is a Hebrew word meaning "the abode of the dead" or "the underworld." For the Hebrews, Sheol was the common destination of both the righteous and the unrighteous after they died. In its earliest form it was not a place of punishment but simply a place where the dead went to dwell after life was finished.

Gehenna
Jesus uses this word twelve times in the Gospels. *Gehenna* is a derivative of *Ge Hinnom*, meaning "Valley of Hinnom" or *Gai ben-Hinnom*, meaning "Valley of Hinnom's Son." Two things were associated with Gehenna at the time Jesus was teaching. First, the valley was a site of a horrible abomination in which children were sacrificed to a god named Moloch. Second, the Valley of Hinnom eventually became the site at which the rubbish of Jerusalem was burned, making it an accursed place for the Jews of Jesus' time.

Hades
Hades is the Greek word traditionally substituted for the Hebrew word *Sheol* in various early translations of the Bible. It was the Hellenistic term for the abode of the dead, the place where all mortals eventually find themselves. The Greeks believed that Hades had many different sections, including the Elysian Fields, which was more like heaven, and Tartarus, which was more like hell. In the context of the New Testament, *Hades* clearly references hell. At only one place in the New Testament, 2 Peter 2:4, is the specific Greek term *Tartarus* actually translated as "hell": "For if God did not spare the angels when they sinned, but cast them into hell and committed them to chains of deepest darkness to be kept until the judgment . . ."

Incidentally, it is an actual place—an old amusement park in New Jersey. This echoes the idea of "hell on earth.")

- How does Jesus describe hell in the parable of the Rich Man and Lazarus (Luke 16:19–31), and what does it reveal about the nature of hell? (The word translated as "hell" in this story, which is unique to Luke's Gospel is *Hades* [see sidebar]. This description of hell is intriguing in many ways. First, it is a Jewish understanding. Traditionally, the poor man Lazarus is being held by the patriarch Abraham. This is the origin of the phrase "rocking my soul in the bosom of Abraham." Lazarus is with Abraham in heaven, and the rich man is in a hell of agony and flames. They are separated by a great chasm but can communicate with each other. The rich man first asks that Abraham send Lazarus with a drop of water "to cool his tongue." Next he asks Abraham to send Lazarus to warn his family of the impending doom. Notice that what put the rich man in hell, his selfishness, is still with him. He asks only that "his tongue be cooled" when we are to assume that there are others suffering with him. He is also self-centered in that he doesn't ask that all people be warned about this torment but only his immediate family. It is this egocentricity that has placed him in hell and is keeping him there. Some scholars suggest that Jesus used this story as a metaphor for the pain and suffering that selfishness and separating ourselves from God can bring to our lives.)

- What do you believe about hell? Is it a literal lake of fire? Is the punishment eternal? Is it about spiritual pain rather than actual physical "fire and brimstone"? (Share the following statistics: According to a recent Harris poll, 82 percent of Americans believe in God, while only 70 percent believe in life after death. Seventy percent believe in the existence of heaven, but only 60 percent believe in hell [*Washington Times*, August 15, 2008]. Why do fewer people believe in hell than heaven? Many Christians struggle with the suggestion that a God of love, grace, and infinite forgiveness would allow any form of eternal punishment to exist. Generally speaking, people want to see evil punished and good rewarded, but that's not actually what hell is about. Actually, winding up in hell is the result of our failure to accept the free gift of grace offered to us by God through Jesus of Nazareth.)

- A commonly held perception of hell is that it is separation from God. Does Psalm 139:7–12 allow for this possibility? (Psalm 139 clearly tells us that it is not possible to be truly separated from God and God's love. "Heaven," "Sheol," "the farthest limits of the sea," even absolute "darkness" cannot hide us from God's loving presence. This would mean that any "separation" we would feel from God would have to be initiated and sustained by us.)

- Explain the play on words found in the title of this episode. Read the quote from John Paul Sartre and the synopsis of his play *No Exit* from the sidebar. How do you feel about the concept of hell on earth? Do we create our own hells? How do you feel about the idea that people might be able to get out of hell (as when the door bursts open)? Is it possible that God might extend the offer of grace beyond our death? (For Bender, hell is literally on earth—in New Jersey, as a matter of fact. Bender is rescued from robot hell by friends who love him. There is actually scriptural support for the idea that God's ultimate goal is to redeem all of creation. Paul says this in Colossians 1:19–20: "For in him all the fullness of God was pleased to dwell, and through him God was pleased to reconcile to himself all things, whether on earth or in heaven, by making peace through the blood of his cross." Paul makes it clear in the verses preceding this that he does mean everything: things in heaven and on earth, things visible and invisible, and thrones and dominions. Are members of your group uncomfortable with the possibility of universal redemption and salvation? If so, why?)

Prayer: God of grace, infinite forgiveness, and eternal love, our desire is that no one should ever end up in a hell after this life or in a self-created hell here and now. Help us to overcome the aspects of our lives that would prevent us from experiencing your unconditional love in all its completeness. Direct us as we seek to live in a spirit of forgiveness rather than a spirit of judgment.

Show us how we can reach out to others through our own unconditional love and encourage them to discover ways that they can
overcome any separation they might feel from you. Let us be their
guides to experiencing the peace that comes from being recon-
ciled to you and embraced in your endless love for all eternity.
Amen.

Something to Talk About: Invite group members to do an infor-
mal survey of the perceptions of hell held by their friends and
family. How do they visualize hell? What do they understand
about hell? How do they feel about hell? Does it frighten them?
Does it confuse them? Do they wish they just didn't have to think
about it at all? When the group meets again, take some time to
have the members share what they discovered.

Family Guy

Eight

Spiritual and Religious Tolerance

Family Guy Episode: "Holy Crap"

Synopsis: Peter's father, Francis, is forced into retirement by his mill. When Peter decides to bring Dad home to live with his family, all hell breaks loose. Francis, a devout Roman Catholic, begins to impose his rigid, judgmental sense of theology and morality on the family. He suggests that Peter should have found a "nice Irish Catholic girl" to marry instead of Lois. Chris and Meg become guilt ridden in response to their grandfather's constant nagging criticism, accusations, and intolerance. In order to get Francis out of the house, Peter arranges a job for his father at the Happy-Go-Lucky Toy Factory, where he works assembling action figures. After being made foreman, Francis fires Peter during an argument about Peter's failures at work and as a father. By fortunate coincidence, the pope is in town for a visit. Peter hijacks the "Popemobile," kidnaps the pope, and enlists his help in convincing Peter's father that he is a good person. In the end, Peter and Francis reconcile, and the pope hires Francis to work "crowd control" for his tour.

Supplementary Reading: *The Gospel according to* The Simpsons, 2nd ed.: Afterword, *Family Guy*, pp. 252–62

Old Testament Lesson: Deut. 5:16

Gospel Lesson: Matt. 7:1–5

85

Root Causes of Religious Intolerance

The Ontario Consultants on Religious Tolerance lists several attitudes, mindsets, and worldviews that can cause religious intolerance (they are condensed and paraphrased in this list):

Fear. We fear what we do not understand completely. Fear breeds intolerance.

Lack of doubt. We have no doubt that we are right and they are wrong, so that settles it.

Monopoly on truth. There is only one truth; we know it, and they don't.

Existence of hell. Hell exists. They're going there; we aren't.

Good versus evil. An "us against them mentality," in which "we" are seen as good and "they" are viewed as evil.

Limited "Golden Rule." Some people believe that "do unto others as you would have them do unto you" applies only to their fellow believers and not to all human beings.

Linking religion and nationalism. Some people or groups create a strong link between their nationality and their religion, to the extent that sometimes they are seen as one and the same.

Collective responsibility. An entire group is held responsible for the hateful actions of one person or a few people.

Blame across generations. An entire group is held responsible for an event that happened generations, centuries, or even millennia ago and is targeted for intolerance.

Passages in a holy text. Some persons believe that passages in a sacred text direct them to be intolerant of other religions and/or denominations.

Religious teachings. More in the past than the present, various religions and denominations taught the necessity of avoiding persons of other faiths.

Epistle Lesson: Eph. 6:1–4

Questions for Discussion: Prior to the discussion, have a member of the group read aloud each of the Scripture lessons.

- In his retirement speech, Francis says to his coworkers, "I just want to say that Jesus loves you. But in my eyes, you're a bunch of sinners and slackers." Why do you think Francis is so intolerant? (Francis believes that there is only one way to salvation and one true church. He believes that he is right and that anyone who doesn't agree with him is wrong. For him this translates into intolerance for any other worldview besides his own. He believes the best way to convert people is to intimidate them and threaten them with hell.)

- How is Francis's intolerance and judgmental attitude expressed to the rest of Peter's family? (He wishes Lois was a "nice Irish Catholic girl." Even when he tries to compliment her he ends up being hurtful and insulting: "You're a good woman, Lois. Perhaps you won't burn in hell after all. Maybe you'll just go to purgatory with all the unbaptized babies." He only reads Stewie the wrathful, judgmental portions of the Bible [which, of course, Stewie loves]. He is convinced that Chris is using the bathroom for "inappropriate behavior," and Chris is overwhelmed with guilt. He accuses Meg of being a "harlot" for holding hands with her boyfriend.)

- Francis despises the fact that Peter and Lois have a "mixed marriage," as Peter is Catholic and Lois is Protestant. Do you know of any mixed marriages between people of different faiths or denominations? How do they handle this issue? (Most contemporary congregations will have several "mixed marriages." Two of the most common types are Catholic-Protestant marriages and "compromise" marriages, which involve spouses from different Protestant denominations who choose a single denomination as a "compromise" so they can both be part of the same spiritual community. Of course, mixed marriages also exist between persons of different religions altogether.)

Ten Ways to Fight Hatred and Intolerance

Teaching Tolerance, a project of the Southern Poverty Law Center, provides a list of ten ways to fight hatred and intolerance:

Act. Do something about hatred and intolerance. Don't ignore it or become apathetic.

Unite. Call a friend, work together, and get others actively involved in ending intolerance.

Support the victims. Victims of intolerance need us to reach out to them in love.

Do your homework. Know the facts behind the problem with which you are dealing.

Create an alternative. Every act of hatred should be met with an act of love and unity.

Speak up. Intolerance and hatred must be acknowledged and denounced.

Lobby leaders. Let your local, state, and national leaders know how you feel about intolerance.

Look long range. Help your community unite to create a future of unity and acceptance.

Teach tolerance. Intolerance, bias, and hatred can be learned. So can love and acceptance.

Dig deeper. Look in your heart for any intolerant tendencies you may have.

- Do you have sympathy for Peter, caught between his loyalty to his wife (which is admittedly shaky in this case) and his wish to please his father? Should Peter allow his father to treat his wife this way, or should he work harder to defend Lois? (It's clear that Peter is completely intimidated by his father and has spent his life desperately seeking his father's affirmation and blessing.

However, it's also obvious that Peter loves Lois very much. When the two come into conflict, it is Lois who loses. [While she acknowledges Francis's insults often, and defends herself against them, she doesn't seem to be that deeply affected by them. Her attitude is one of reluctant acceptance. That's just the way Francis is, and he is not likely to change.] This is definitely not fair to Lois, but Peter is so desperate for his father's love and acceptance that he allows the situation to persist. By the end of the episode he is finally willing to stand up to his father for the first time.)

- Have you experienced this kind of religious intolerance? What forms did it take? (Many Christians will emphasize the idea that only Christians will enter heaven. For some this leads to a self-righteous and highly judgmental view of others. Persons of other faiths can also reflect this intolerance back to Christians. Other Christians demonstrate an intolerance of all denominations or groups except their own—the idea that "if you're not Christian like I'm Christian, you're not Christian at all.")

- How do you feel about this kind of religious intolerance? Do you think it makes a difference in other people's lives? (This will be a matter of personal opinion; however, most of us do not appreciate intolerance, being judged, or attitudes that define us in a negative way.)

- Did you know that for more than a century after the Protestant Reformation, Protestants and Catholics in Europe waged brutal wars against one another, even burning "heretics" at the stake? In Ireland, in particular, wars between native Catholics (like the Griffiths' ancestors) and English Protestants (under Oliver Cromwell and King William of Orange) were especially savage and are still remembered today in the contemporary conflicts between the Irish and the British. How do you think people justified this as "Christians"? (After the group has discussed this for a few minutes, share the list of "Root Causes of Religious Intolerance" with them. It should be obvious that all of these are represented in the conflicts between these two groups. If you would like to extend this discussion, have the group talk about the historical animosity of many Christians toward Muslims and Jews. Be aware that this is a current "hot button" issue and you will need to guide the group in being open-minded, tolerant, and accepting.)

- What do you think is the answer to expressions of religious intolerance? (Emphasis should be placed on the unconditional love and infinite forgiveness of God rather than focusing on condemnation and judgment. In Luke 7:1–2 Jesus says, "Do not judge, so that you may not be judged. For with the judgment you make you will be judged, and the measure you give will be the measure you get." We should emphasize acceptance and grace rather than fear and threats of eternal punishment.)

- How does Jesus address the problem of judgmental intolerance in Luke 7:1–5? (Many scholars believe that this is an example of Jesus teaching by telling a "joke," or at least using humor. The image Jesus creates is of a person with a log in his or her eye trying to get a gnat out of someone else's eye. Jesus' teachings against being judgmental are straightforward and clear. Judgmental attitudes are the foundation of intolerance and often lead to anger, hatred, and violence.)

- Francis tells Meg that God will strike her "sinful heart with leprosy" for holding her boyfriend's hand. He also suggests that an episode of *The Dick Van Dyke Show* ends when "Laura burns the roast and God kills her for parading her bum around in those pants." Do you think God punishes us for our sins in this life? (You may actually have persons in the group who believe this. A God of love would not use diseases to punish us because we behave inappropriately. Threatening those we judge with the idea that God might punish them in this wrathful way is one of the most hateful things we can do.)

- When Peter kidnaps the pope to mediate his family's problems, the pope actually supports Peter by telling Francis he has raised a "fine son." How does he react? What does this say about his attitude toward authority? (Francis is so wrapped up in his judgmental attitudes that he refuses to accept an affirmation of Peter even if it comes from the pope. One of the key problems with intolerance is that people will often reject any spiritual authority in order to persist in their judgments of others.)

- How do Deuteronomy 5:16 and Ephesians 6:1–4 speak to Peter's relationship with his dad? (The commandment to "Honor your father and mother" expresses the need to give parents the respect they deserve. However, God would never want us to honor destructive attitudes or behaviors. The passage from Ephesians takes this one step further by insisting that respect between parent and child should be reciprocal. Children should love and respect their parents, and parents should love and respect their children in return.)

- When Peter tells his father he loves him but doesn't like him, the pope tells Peter, "The good Lord said, 'Honor thy father.' He never said anything about liking him." Can we love someone without liking him or her? (The foundation of truly unconditional love is to love others "in spite of themselves." In Luke 6:35–37 Jesus teaches, "Love your enemies, do good, and lend, expecting nothing in return. Your reward will be great, and you will be children of the Most High, for he is kind to the ungrateful and the wicked. Be merciful, just as your Father is merciful. 'Do not judge, and you will not be judged; do not condemn, and you will not be condemned. Forgive, and you will be forgiven.'" We usually don't like our enemies, but Jesus commands us to love them. In fact, Jesus even suggests that the forgiveness we receive is contingent on the forgiveness we give to others. We don't have to "like" certain people, including what they say or do, in order to love them. That is where tolerance begins.)

- In a subsequent episode, Francis dies and on his deathbed remains harshly critical of Peter, rather than loving and accepting him. Is it possible that, regardless of experience and the hope and prayers of others, some people simply will not (or cannot) change? (Christians believe that grace can change anything. However, each individual has to accept grace for herself and choose to live a life of unconditional love, forgiveness, and tolerance. While this is the ideal, there seem to be many people who don't think they need to change or simply refuse to change. All we can do is nurture them with love and prayers and hope for the best. We can never know what will motivate someone to begin the process of transformational change through grace.)

Prayer: Merciful God, You made all of the people of the world in your own image and placed before us the pathway of salvation through different preachers who claimed to have been your saints and prophets. But the contradictions in their teachings and interpretations of them have resulted in creating divisions, hatreds, and bloodshed in the world community. Millions of innocent men, women, and children have so far been brutally killed by the militants of several religions who have been committing horrifying crimes against humanity, and millions more will be butchered by them in the future if you do not help us find ways to reunite peacefully. In the name of God, the compassionate, the merciful, look with compassion on the whole human family; take away the controversial teachings of arrogance, divisions, and hatreds which have badly infected our hearts; break down the walls that separate us; reunite us in bonds of love; and work through our struggle and confusion to accomplish Your purposes on earth; that, in Your good time, all nations and races may jointly serve You in justice, peace and harmony. Amen. (This is a Muslim prayer for unity and peace that is prayed by the Movement for Reforming Society in Lahore, Pakistan.)

Something to Talk About: These three Web sites provide extensive resources for discussing and dealing with religious intolerance: http://www.tolerance.org (Teaching Tolerance), http://www.religioustolerance.org (Ontario Consultants on Religious Tolerance), and http://www.center2000.org (Center for Reduction of Religious-Based Conflict).

If you would like to expand this session to a retreat, here are two excellent movies that deal with the issues and attitudes surrounding the theme of intolerance.

- *Saved* (2004, 92 minutes, PG-13). Mary (Jena Malone) is a "good" Christian girl who attends a "good" Christian high school with many "good" Christian friends. Her best friend, Hilary Faye (Mandy Moore), is the most popular and powerful girl in the school. Mary seems to have the perfect Christian boyfriend, Dean (Chad Faust)—until she discovers that Dean may be gay. After receiving a vision of Jesus in the swimming pool, she decides to dedicate herself to keeping Dean straight by offering him her virginity. The plan backfires when Mary becomes pregnant and Dean is sent off to a "degayification" center. When Hilary conspires to make Mary a pariah at the school, Mary finds real friendship with the school's misfits—Cassandra (Eva Amurri), the school's only Jewish girl; Roland (Macaulay Culkin), Hilary's wheelchair-bound brother; and Patrick (Patrick Fugit), the skateboarding son of the school's principal, Pastor Skip (Martin Donovan).

- *School Ties* (1992, 106 minutes, PG-13). Set in the 1950s, *School Ties* is a story of prejudice and anti-Semitism at an elite boys academy. David Green (Brendan Fraser) is a superior athlete from a working class background who is admitted to the school as a football star. David wants to attend Harvard, and the students and administrators at the school want to win football championships. Things are going well until Charlie Dillon (Matt Damon), a bigoted, spoiled, and arrogant classmate discovers that David is a Jew. Once David's secret is revealed he is reviled and persecuted by the other boys. When Charlie cheats on his exams he blames it on David, and the community must choose to support one over the other.

King of the Hill

Nine

Talking about God

King of the Hill Episode: "Are You There, God?
It's Me, Margaret Hill"

Synopsis: Peggy can't find a full-time teaching job and is starting to get discouraged. Hank suggests that Peggy come to work with him at Strickland Propane, something she does only reluctantly. Once at Strickland's, all her worst fears are confirmed. Peggy then hears about a full-time teaching job at a Catholic school. The only catch is that she has to be a nun. Desperate, Peggy borrows a habit from a supply closet and poses as a nun. She loves her new job until the mother superior is called for jury duty and asks Peggy to teach her Catholic doctrine class. All Peggy knows about the Catholic Church comes from watching a sleazy cable channel action show about a crime-fighting priest. She decides to improvise and leads the class in a free-form discussion of the questions the students have about their faith and beliefs. Peggy has a dream in which her students are sent to hell because they haven't been taught the correct doctrines (the fires of hell are fueled by Strickland propane supplied by Hank, of course). Feeling guilty about her deception, Peggy strips off the habit and confesses to the mother superior that she is actually a Methodist. Having lost her teaching job, Peggy returns to Strickland Propane to work with Hank, only to be fired by her own husband when Hank realizes that teaching is her true calling and that she will never be happy selling propane.

Supplementary Reading: *The Gospel According to* The Simpsons, 2nd ed.: Afterword, *King of the Hill*, pp. 235–52

Old Testament Lesson: Ps. 89:1–2

New Testament Lesson: 1 John 1:1–4

Activity: Explain to the group members that they have suddenly been thrust into a time in which being a Christian is forbidden. They are not allowed to have Bibles, prayer books, litanies, hymnals, or any other resource that describes what they believe in detail. What could they reconstruct from their memories about Christian theology and the specific beliefs of their church or denomination? On a whiteboard or flip chart, make a list of each point members make. After about five minutes have everyone consider the list. Was it more difficult than they expected? Could they remember specifics? How did they remember what they

---

Are You There, God? It's Me, Margaret

The title for this episode of *King of the Hill* is an homage to one of the best, most popular, and most enduring young adult novels ever written. The groundbreaking *Are You There, God? It's Me, Margaret*, by Judy Blume, was first published in 1970. The novel centers on the trials and tribulations of a sixth-grade girl who is growing up without religion, or better stated, between religions. Margaret has a Jewish father and a Christian mother, and the novel focuses on her search for the religion that will be best for her. Along the way, Margaret also deals with other preteen issues, including anticipating her first menstrual cycle, purchasing her first bra, and handling boy problems and the jealousy of other girls. She longs to have a deeper relationship with God and talks with God about all of her concerns and decisions. The title of the book comes from the sentence with which Margaret begins each of her prayers.

listed? After this exercise, do they feel that they need to understand the details of their church or denominations' beliefs more completely?

Questions for Discussion: Prior to the discussion, have a member of the group read aloud each of the Scripture lessons.

- How do you feel about Peggy's decision to impersonate a nun in order to get her teaching job? (While what Peggy does is obviously wrong, we may sympathize with her passion and desire to teach. She is clearly an excellent teacher, and at first it seems like a harmless deception.)

- How does Peggy's deception catch up with her? (When the mother superior is called to jury duty, she asks Peggy to teach her Principles of Catholicism class. The mother superior assumes that Peggy has the theological training to teach this class because she is a nun. Peggy accepts but has no idea what she is doing. In fact, she isn't even sure how to make the sign of the cross.)

- What is Peggy's first challenge in teaching this class? (When she asks what they have been studying, one of the students replies, "Transubstantiation." Transubstantiation is a theological term that describes the change that takes place in the bread and wine into the body and blood of Jesus Christ during the sacrament of Communion. This theological point presents one of the significant differences between the Roman Catholic Church and the Protestant churches. Most Protestants hold a theological position called "consubstantiation," which states that the sacrament of Communion is symbolic and memorial in nature and that the bread and wine communicate the presence of Christ in a mystical way. Peggy doesn't understand this, and that means she can't teach it to her students.)

- How does Peggy respond to this challenge? (She has told the mother superior that religion is not her subject. Rather than addressing the theology she is supposed to be teaching, she suggests that she and the class "just rap about God." She leads

Talking about God 101

Theology. Anselm of Canterbury once defined theology as "faith seeking understanding." Formed from two Greek roots, *theos* (God) and *logos* (word), theology is the study of religious faith and practice in an attempt to understand God and God's relationship to creation.

Doctrine. The ordered presentation of a body of theological teachings, principles, and positions that describes the theology held by a particular church or denomination.

Dogma. A body of doctrines formally stated and authoritatively proclaimed by a church or denomination that is not to be disputed, doubted, or diverged from in any way.

Orthodoxy. Formed from two Greek roots, *ortho* (correct) and *dox* (thought), orthodoxy is the collection of foundationally established beliefs, theology, and doctrines considered to be correctly presented and absolutely authoritative by a church or denomination.

Heresy. An alternative theological point of view from what is considered orthodox by a church or denomination. Heresy dissents from the generally accepted understanding of beliefs and theological standards held as authoritative by a community of faith.

Confession of faith. A creedal statement of the fundamental beliefs and/or articles of faith of a church or denomination. In many churches a confession of faith is the statement of a set of doctrinal positions and standards that must be held by all members of that community. Confessions of faith are intended to simplify the doctrines of a church and present them in a unified and complete form so they can be taught easily to members.

Systematic theology. A well-organized, methodical presentation of the beliefs held by a religion in a way that demonstrates how those beliefs are relative to a particular context or time. A complete Christian systematic theology will seek to answer questions such as: Who is God? Who is Jesus Christ? Who is the Holy Spirit? How is God revealed? How should human beings relate to God?

the class in a free form discussion of their questions about theology. She improvises her answers, and the students love the
freedom they have to discuss what's on their minds rather than
rigidly following a text.)

- What are the advantages and disadvantages of Peggy's style of
teaching theology? (The students love the question-and-answer
style. One student asks, "Does God have a last name?" Peggy
replies, "No, he only has one name, like Cher." Another student inquires, "If cats can't pray do they still go to heaven?"
Peggy answers, "I heard somewhere that all dogs go to heaven,
so I'm sure that cats do not. Keep 'em coming. Let's play
'Stump the Sister.'" The students are fully involved and having
fun learning, but Peggy has no idea what she is talking about in
relationship to Catholic theology. As young Catholics her students are supposed to be learning the correct understanding of
Catholic doctrine. Peggy responds to their questions from her
heart, but she's flying by the seat of her pants when it comes to
any real understanding of theology.)

- Have you ever heard any of your friends say, "I'm spiritual but
not religious"? What do you think they mean? Is that possible?
How important do you think it is to hold a formal set of beliefs?
(When people say, "I'm spiritual but not religious," they most
often mean that their spirituality is an internalized commitment rather than a matter of outward religious practice. This
idea is often expressed as a rationalization for not participating
in some [or all] of a religious community's traditions as well as
rejecting some [or all] of that community's doctrines. People
who share this sentiment usually place a high value on personal
experience as the foundation of their spiritual commitment and
are uncomfortable with the idea of an institution dictating their
theological understanding and beliefs.)

- What helps Peggy to see the gravity of what she is doing? (In the
teachers lounge she notices that the other teachers are watching
the cable show about the crime-fighting priest and criticizing it
for its "bad theology." Peggy suggests that "whatever gets people
talking about Catholicism is a good thing," to which one of the

sisters replies, "Our children's souls are at stake. If the children are confused with a lot of nonsense they may lose their faith, and you know how God punishes that—eternal damnation." This shocks Peggy and gets her thinking.)

- How do you feel about the sister's argument that being confused about theology may lead to loss of faith and eternal damnation? (While we should always seek to know and understand more about our faith and theology, most people believe a loving God would not send us to hell simply for being confused about what we believe. Our acceptance of God's grace is much more important than what we know about theological details.)

- When Hank discovers Peggy's deception he says, "You would rather live a lie than sell an honest day's gas?" Does this convince Peggy that what she is doing is wrong? (Peggy is willing to rationalize the fact that she is impersonating a nun in order to be able to do what she truly loves—teach. She hasn't completely thought through the implications of what she is doing.)

- What does Psalm 89:1–2 have to say about theology? (Before theology and beliefs were written down, the Hebrew people shared the stories of God and their interpretations of God's actions in the world through an oral tradition. Imagine sitting around a fire at the end of a long day and listening to a storyteller. The psalmist says, "I will sing of your steadfast love, O LORD, forever; with my mouth I will proclaim your faithfulness to all generations. I declare that your steadfast love is established forever; your faithfulness is as firm as the heavens." Poetry and song were used by the Hebrew people to teach, remember, and communicate their theology. An oversimplified example of this would be teaching children to sing "Jesus Loves Me" or "I Am the Church, You Are the Church." Books from the Hebrew Bible such as Psalms, Job, Proverbs, and Ecclesiastes are referred to by scholars as "Wisdom literature" because they begin a long tradition of thinking theologically about God's relationship to creation.)

Prayer: O God our God, grant us grace to desire you with a whole heart, so that desiring you we may seek and find you; and so finding you, may love you; and loving you, we may hate those sins that separate us from you, for the sake of Jesus Christ. Amen. (This is one of the most famous prayers of St. Anselm of Canterbury, who first defined theology as "faith seeking understanding.")

Something to Talk About: Have enough copies of your church's or denomination's articles of faith on hand so that each member of the group can have a copy. (If you don't know where to find them, consult your pastor.) Have each person in the group choose one or two of the questions from the list provided in the box describing systematic theology. Challenge the members of the group to research the questions they have chosen using the articles of faith as their only source document. When you gather again, have them share what they have learned. Was it what they expected? Did anything surprise them? Do they agree with what they found?

CPSIA information can be obtained
at www.ICGtesting.com
Printed in the USA
LVHW111603140821
695327LV00009B/1182